LOCAL CURRENCY COLLATERAL FOR CROSS-BORDER FINANCIAL TRANSACTIONS

POLICY RECOMMENDATIONS FROM THE CROSS-BORDER SETTLEMENT INFRASTRUCTURE FORUM

SEPTEMBER 2022

ASIAN DEVELOPMENT BANK

ADB

Notes:
ADB recognizes "China" as the People's Republic of China; "Hong Kong" as Hong Kong, China; "Korea" as the Republic
of Korea; and "Vietnam" as Viet Nam.

In this report, international standards for naming conventions—International Organization for Standardization (ISO)
3166 for country codes and ISO 4217 for currency codes—are used to reflect the discussions of the Cross-Border
Settlement Infrastructure Forum to improve cross-border bond and cash settlement infrastructures in the region.
ASEAN+3 comprises the Association of Southeast Asian Nations (ASEAN) plus the People's Republic of China, Japan,
and the Republic of Korea.

The economies of ASEAN+3 as defined in ISO 3166 include Brunei Darussalam (BN; BRN); Cambodia (KH; KHM);
the People's Republic of China (CN; CHN); Hong Kong, China (HK; HKG); Indonesia (ID; IDN); Japan (JP; JPN);
the Republic of Korea (KR; KOR); the Lao People's Democratic Republic (LA; LAO); Malaysia (MY; MYS); Myanmar
(MM; MMR); the Philippines (PH; PHL); Singapore (SG; SGP); Thailand (TH; THA); and Viet Nam (VN; VNM).
The currencies of ASEAN+3 as defined in ISO 4217 include the Brunei dollar (BND), Cambodian riel (KHR),
Chinese renminbi (CNY), Hong Kong dollar (HKD), Indonesian rupiah (IDR), Japanese yen (JPY), Korean won (KRW),
Lao kip (LAK), Malaysian ringgit (MYR), Myanmar kyat (MMK), Philippine peso (PHP), Singapore dollar (SGD),
Thai baht (THB), and Vietnamese dong (VND).

Cover design by Francis Joseph M. Manio.

CONTENTS

TABLES, FIGURES, AND BOX

TABLES

FIGURES

BOX

STATEMENT FROM THE CROSS-BORDER SETTLEMENT INFRASTRUCTURE FORUM CHAIR

Wider use of local-currency-denominated bonds for cross-border collateral transactions would serve as a key enabler for the development of regional bond markets by alleviating the collateral costs of financial institutions and expanding market liquidity. Therefore, without collective efforts to ensure that collateral is actively used across the region, the development of cross-border financial transactions will continue to be limited. This report, *Local Currency Collateral for Cross-Border Financial Transactions*, proposes seven policy recommendations with a view to achieving this ambitious goal in the Association of Southeast Asian Nations plus the People's Republic of China, Japan, and the Republic of Korea (ASEAN+3) region.

As the acting chair and vice-chair of the Cross-Border Settlement Infrastructure Forum (CSIF), I would like to express my gratitude to the CSIF members and observers for their contributions to the completion of this report. I also look forward to the ongoing support from CSIF members and observers for this project since it is presently in the first stage of implementing the objectives of the Asian Bond Markets Initiative, which is promoting the use of local currency bonds for cross-border collateral transactions. The acting chair also wishes to thank the Asian Development Bank Secretariat and consultants for providing valuable input for the report.

SEUNG-KWON LEE
Acting Chair, CSIF
Vice-Chair, CSIF
Director, Clearing and Settlement Department
Korea Securities Depository

ACKNOWLEDGMENTS

The Asian Development Bank (ADB), as Secretariat of the Cross-Border Settlement Infrastructure Forum (CSIF), would like to express its sincere gratitude to the vice-chair for coordinating relevant discussions as well as to members and observers for providing input for *Local Currency Collateral for Cross-Border Financial Transactions*.

This report was written in view of (i) examining the current status of regional bond markets, (ii) providing the Association of Southeast Asian Nations plus the People's Republic of China, Japan, and the Republic of Korea (ASEAN+3) member economies with policy recommendations for fostering the use of local currency bonds for cross-border collateral transactions, and (iii) suggesting effective ways to enact such recommendations. This paper was prepared mainly by Leelark Park, an ADB consultant, with support from the ADB Secretariat of the CSIF—led by Satoru Yamadera, along with Byung-Wook Ahn, Kosintr Puonfsophol, and Yvonne Osonia, as well as other ADB consultants, Matthias Schmidt, Ki-Hoon Ro, and Taiji Inui—to lay the foundation for boosting the development of domestic bond markets as well as cross-border collateral transactions in the region.

CSIF members provided input by answering questionnaires and conducting a comprehensive review of this draft report. Observing authorities and market experts kindly shared their knowledge and experience of the collateral market and its related constraints. Furthermore, the smooth organization of multiple online meetings made the intensive discussions possible. The ADB Secretariat expresses its heartfelt gratitude to the region's central banks, central securities depositories, and other authorities participating as observers. Without such strong support and cooperation from CSIF members and other relevant institutions within the region, this report would not have been possible.

No part of this report represents the official view of any institution that participated as a CSIF member or observer. The CSIF Secretariat bears the sole responsibility for the contents of this report.

ABBREVIATIONS

ABIF	ASEAN Banking Integration Framework
ADB	Asian Development Bank
ASEAN	Association of Southeast Asian Nations
ASEAN+3	Association of Southeast Asian Nations plus the People's Republic of China, Japan, and the Republic of Korea
BIS	Bank for International Settlements
BNM	Bank Negara Malaysia
BOJ	Bank of Japan
BOJ-NET	Bank of Japan Financial Network System
BOT	Bank of Thailand
BSP	Bangko Sentral ng Pilipinas (Central Bank of the Philippines)
CBCA	cross-border collateral arrangement
CCBM	correspondent central banking model
CCDC	China Central Depository & Clearing Co., Ltd.
CCP	central clearing counterparty
CSD	central securities depository
CSIF	Cross-Border Settlement Infrastructure Forum
DVP	delivery-versus-payment
ECB	European Central Bank
FCY	foreign currency
FMI	financial market infrastructure
HQLA	high-quality liquid assets
ICSD	international central securities depository
IOSCO	International Organization of Securities Commissions
LCY	local currency
MAS	Monetary Authority of Singapore
OTC	over-the-counter
PFMI	Principles for Financial Market Infrastructures
QABs	Qualified ASEAN Banks
RTGS	real-time gross settlement
SSS	securities settlement system
USD	United States dollar

EXECUTIVE SUMMARY

Financial integration and interconnectedness is making significant progress not only in global financial markets but also in the Association of Southeast Asian Nations plus the People's Republic of China, Japan, and the Republic of Korea (ASEAN+3) region. In parallel, global regulatory initiatives have led to environmental changes in capital markets in the domain of collateral transactions. Securing and utilizing eligible collateral in cross-border financial transactions is also considered an important competence in financial stability. Consequently, the role of bonds as collateral is on a growth trend and the significance of high-quality liquid bonds in financial transactions is increasing.

Bond markets serve as the basis for supporting the financial market overall where the immunity of bonds to credit risk is one of the key enablers for the smooth functioning of financial intermediation. In addition, well-established market infrastructure in one economy can be linked with market infrastructures across economies, thereby efficiently supporting cross-border bond transactions.

In the ASEAN+3 region, the issuance of local currency (LCY) bonds has been steadily increasing, driven mainly by the economic growth and the policy actions of each member economy. However, the trading volume of bonds has not shown a notable increase in the secondary market. Furthermore, while domestic market infrastructures are being put in place, the cases of infrastructure linkages for cross-border clearing and settlement of bonds are limited. As a result, the region's collateral markets are still in the development phase and do not play a major role in cross-border financial transactions.

If cross-border collateral transactions were to notably increase in the region, the LCY bond market's development, market participants' more effective risk management through a wider range of hedging tools, and their financial cost reduction might all be possible. Moreover, the vitalization of collateral transactions across the region might expand market liquidity, diversify financial instruments, and contribute to regional financial stability.

Cross-border collateral arrangements (CBCAs) could, in particular, increase the cross-border use of high-quality bonds such as government bonds that are denominated in domestic currencies. It additionally could contribute to increasing liquidity in the bond market. For this reason, in the euro area, national central banks are extensively using CBCAs with various models. However, in the ASEAN+3 region, the CBCAs that have been adopted by some regional central banks are rarely used, suggesting some structural challenges in scaling up the arrangements.

The development of cross-border collateral markets in ASEAN+3 has been affected by a number of factors. To identify the issues in the region, this study conducted a survey targeting Cross-Border Settlement Infrastructure Forum (CSIF) member institutions. The survey responses and additional information from the public and industry experts show that there exists a series of constraints in the region to the circulation of high-quality bonds as collateral. These include the lack of a domestic bond market basis, insufficient public disclosure of relevant laws and regulations, foreign exchange-related restrictions and constraints, insufficient market infrastructures for cross-border transactions, and limited disclosure of relevant market information.

Whether the use of LCY bonds can have overall benefits depends on a number of factors such as the regulatory frameworks, the environment of the domestic financial market, and cross-border market infrastructures. Furthermore, to facilitate cross-border collateral transactions, a number of other factors need to be taken into account. These range from systemic risks, regulatory frameworks, capacities of central bank business and market infrastructures, and market interdependency.

In addition, active use of LCY bonds for cross-border collateral transactions could help the development of the regional bond market by reducing the credit costs of financial institutions and expanding market liquidity.

Against this backdrop, this report proposes seven policy recommendations for promoting the cross-border use of LCY bonds as collateral in the ASEAN+3 region:

1. **Further development of local currency bond markets.** A well-functioning domestic bond market is one of the key stepping-stones for supporting efficient cross-border collateral transactions. Thus, the region's LCY bond markets need to be further developed as the first step. In particular, it is necessary to first seek ways to develop domestic interbank bond markets across economies in the region. This is because the interbank bond market—in which financial institutions, banks in particular, participate—could lead to the development of the cross-border collateral market as well as a whole new bond market.

2. **Disclosure enhancement of regulatory frameworks and market information.** The disclosure of key market information, including the transaction and settlement status of bond transactions, would be a critical enabler for the active use of cross-border collateral upon LCY bonds. Both the *ASEAN+3 Bond Market Guides* and *AsianBondsOnline* are good channels for foreign investors to collect relevant information about the region. It would, however, also be desirable for each economy to disclose pertinent information in a more comprehensive and transparent manner, particularly with regard to regulatory frameworks and market information, through their own respective platforms.

3. **Enhancement of market infrastructures.** Cross-border collateral transactions are heavily dependent upon an efficient and flexible collateral management scheme supported by stable operations of financial market infrastructures. They include well-functioning central securities depositories and securities settlement systems, delivery-versus-payment arrangements being in place, and the wider introduction of international technical standards. Therefore, it is imperative to enhance domestic market infrastructures.

4. **Wider linkages between regional market infrastructures.** To promote the use of LCY bonds for cross-border collateral transactions in ASEAN+3, linkages among the region's market infrastructures might need to be expanded. The wider linkage network would support swift mobilization of LCY bonds across individual markets, alleviate transaction costs, strengthen interoperability, and better manage operational risk via straight-through-processing.

5. **Expansion of central banks' role in cross-border collateral management.** The impact of central bank collateral frameworks on cross-border transactions—including collateral availability, bond prices, and market practices—is of critical significance. In particular, central bank policy measures that assess and decide on asset eligibility, haircut ratios, and accessibility to counterparties can have a decisive impact on collateral management practices. Thus, the role of central banks for promoting cross-border collateral transactions needs to be expanded.

6. **Expansion of cross-border collateral arrangements.** CBCAs suggest there is potential for increasing market liquidity in bond markets, promoting the use of LCY bonds for cross-border collateral transactions, and contributing to the strengthening of financial stability. Therefore, ASEAN+3 member economies need to develop measures to facilitate CBCAs. Critical issues such as central bank's risk management burden, legal uncertainties, and higher funding costs should be addressed carefully when CBCAs are under consideration.

7. **Facilitation of Qualified ASEAN Banks.** Given the nature of Qualified ASEAN Banks (QABs), they can have a positive effect on the increased incidence of cross-border collateral transactions, while the reverse might also be true in that those transactions might be a catalyst for more active use of QABs in the region. If, in particular, QABs are put in place in conjunction with CBCAs, the adoption of cross-border collateral transactions involving LCY bonds might be further accelerated. Thus, greater market access and improved operational flexibility for QABs need to be further considered.

In parallel, this study proposes follow-up actions to be taken to further develop the regional cross-border collateral market. These next steps include (i) additional in-depth studies on the subject of cross-border collateral financing, repurchase agreements, and other derivatives transactions, as well as the comparative analysis of central bank's repo operations; (ii) support for market participants' activities; (iii) establishment of ASEAN+3 regional market and legal practices; (iv) close cooperation between authorities and related agencies for the expansion of regional cross-border financing and financial stability; and (v) establishment of working groups for constructing a road map.

I

INTRODUCTION

Financial integration and interconnectedness is making significant progress not only in global financial markets but also in the Association of Southeast Asian Nations plus the People's Republic of China, Japan, and the Republic of Korea (ASEAN+3) region. In parallel, global regulatory initiatives have led to environmental changes in capital markets, particularly in the domain of collateral transactions. Consequently, the role of bonds as collateral suggests a growth trend is in place and the significance of high-quality liquid bonds, government bonds in particular, in financial transactions is on the rise. The region's bond markets are well developed overall, particularly their sizable primary markets, but the markets of some member economies are still considered to be in their infancy. Most bond issuances remain in the domestic currency, and the role of local currency (LCY) bonds as collateral for cross-border financial transactions is still confined within the region's boundaries.

As the financial system in the region has long relied on a bank-oriented indirect financing, the regional capital market as a direct financing channel is relatively less developed considering the overall size of funding operations. The total foreign exchange reserves of ASEAN+3 economies accounted for 49% of the global total at the end of 2020.[1] Also, according to the investment portfolio statistics of the International Monetary Fund (IMF) (Table 1), among ASEAN+3's total overseas investments, those in the United States (US) and European markets comprised 64.1% of the region's total overseas investments at the end of 2020. On the contrary, only 11.4% of the region's foreign investment was made by regional economies. Although this proportion shows a significant increase from only 3.7% in 2005, it remains very low in the absolute context.

Table 1: ASEAN+3 Investment Portfolio
(USD billion)

Year	Advanced Economy				ASEAN+3		Total
	US	Europe	Amount	%	Amount	%	
2005	660	789	1,449	68.5	78	3.7	2,119
2010	1,017	1,124	2,141	63.4	209	6.2	3,378
2020	1,821	1,125	2,946	64.1	523	11.4	4,595

ASEAN+3 = Association of Southeast Asian Nations plus the People's Republic of China, Japan, and the Republic of Korea; US = United States; USD = United States dollar.

Source: International Monetary Fund. Coordinated Portfolio Investment Survey. https://data.imf.org/.

---

[1] Foreign exchange reserves of the world and ASEAN+3 was USD12,701 billion and USD6,250 billion, respectively, at the end of 2020 per the *ASEAN+3 Regional Economic Outlook 2021* and the IMF's *Currency Composition of Official Foreign Exchange Reserves 2020*.

As such, regional funds are being invested mainly in the markets of the US and Europe, and these funds are being reinvested back into the region, which disguises the true picture of regional investments. The excessive reliance on assets denominated in foreign currency (FCY) further poses a risk of exposure to changes in external economic turbulence. Therefore, to promote regional investments and support further growth of the local capital markets, bond market development based on high-quality assets is of critical importance.

Since the global financial crisis, financial regulations have been strengthened worldwide, making the risk of unsecured financial transactions more recognizable. Securing and utilizing eligible collateral in cross-border financial transactions, in particular, is considered an important competence in financial stability.

Meanwhile, the clearing and settlement infrastructures for supporting cross-border collateral transactions are still insufficient and therefore most asset investment and risk management depends on global market infrastructures, which seems one of the main factors explaining the repetition of shocks to the regional financial system transmitted from economies beyond the regional borders.

One of the most typical financial transactions involving securities collateral is the repurchase agreement (repo). While the region's central banks' repo transactions for monetary policy implementation are large in size, market-based repo transactions and cross-border repo transactions are understood to be negligible in regional markets. Furthermore, the eligible cross-border collateral pool normally comprises bonds issued by major countries like the US and European countries, and most of bonds issued by ASEAN+3 member economies are rarely traded and are not accepted as eligible collateral in the global market.

There have been policy and technical dialogues around the four task forces under the Asian Bond Markets Initiatives, with the aim of invigorating regional bond market development. However, the activation of cross-border collateral transactions should be supported by the development of pertinent markets such as repo transactions. In particular, these transactions are expected to increase available collateral, thereby supporting the liquidity of individual markets while reducing the risk of systemic impacts. Government bonds from a practical standpoint play a crucial role in the smooth operations of the capital market based on the general market perception of their immunity against credit risk.

Since this study is aimed at activating the use of LCY bonds for cross-border financial transactions, one of the measures to facilitate the regional bond market, which focuses only on bonds as collateral, was analyzed. Bonds, especially government bonds, are recognized as safe assets due to their high credit ratings and large trading volumes, making them suitable for collateral transactions. In addition, most central banks include high-quality liquid bonds as eligible assets when providing liquidity to banks.

This report first seeks to identify constraints associated with cross-border collateral transactions in the view that the increase in the use of LCY bonds could be a means of mitigating risk by expanding market liquidity. To this end, this study conducted a survey of member institutions of the Cross-Border Settlement Infrastructure Forum (CSIF) (see Appendix 2 for questionnaires).

Based on the survey results and information from the public and industry experts, the report presents policy recommendations to promote cross-border collateral transactions, as well as LCY-denominated bond markets in general, by making active use of high-quality bonds. Lastly, the report proposes follow-up actions to be taken in the future to further develop regional collateral markets.

II

OVERVIEW OF THE COLLATERAL MARKET ENVIRONMENT IN THE REGION

A. Bond Issuances and Transactions

1. Primary Market

In general, the level of development of the bond market, as compared to the bank-oriented indirect financial market, is considered to be an indicator measuring the degree of financial market development. The bond market requires well-functioning financial market infrastructure in relation to clearing and settlement, along with investor diversity.

The amount of LCY bond issuances in the ASEAN+3 region has been steadily increasing, driven mainly by the economic growth and policy efforts of each member economy. In particular, regional issuance has shown a more notable increase since 2015, demonstrating a sixfold surge from USD5.4 trillion in 2001 to USD32.2 trillion in 2020, when the region's total issuance increased by 19.2% compared to 2019. This growing trend of issuances was bolstered mainly by government bonds, accounting for 71.8% of the total issuances at USD23.1 trillion, which is a significantly higher proportion than that of corporate bonds, including commercial bank bonds, which made up 26.5% of the total (Figure 1).[2]

However, in terms of volume, bond issuance in ASEAN+3 in 2020 was driven largely by only a few regional economies, with issuance volumes in other economies remaining marginal (Figure 2). That said, the relative size of bond issuances against gross domestic product shows a slightly different picture, as some member economies with low absolute volumes of issuance have relatively higher proportions as a share of gross domestic product. Thus, the absolute size of the bond market in some member economies is small, but it is larger when accounting for the economy's overall size (Figure 3).

The LCY bond market of emerging economies has been continuously developing in recent years. For instance, some Association of Southeast Asian Nations (ASEAN) countries initiated the development of a sustainable bond market intended for green, social, and sustainability bonds. This initiative provides investors an opportunity to support sustainable regional growth and demand for green investments.

---

[2] Issuance data are for 10 economies among the ASEAN+3 grouping: the People's Republic of China; Hong Kong, China; Indonesia; Japan; the Republic of Korea; Malaysia; the Philippines; Singapore; Thailand; and Viet Nam.

Figure 1: Local Currency Bond Issuances in ASEAN+3
(USD billion)

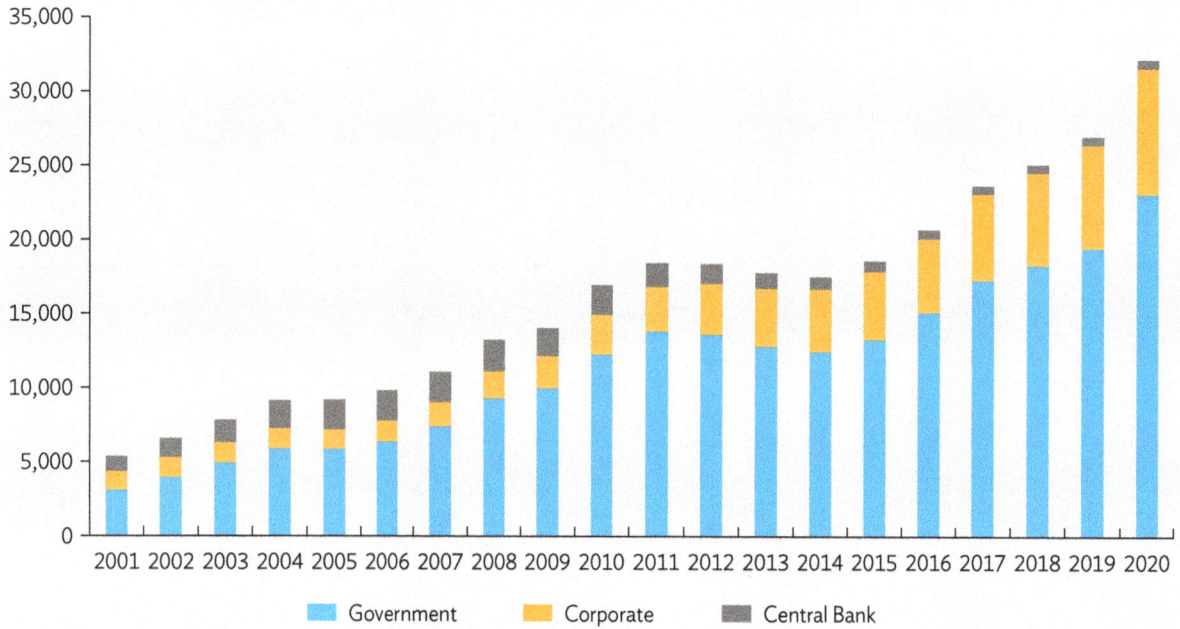

ASEAN+3 = Association of Southeast Asian Nations plus the People's Republic of China, Japan, and the Republic of Korea; USD = United States dollar.

Source: ADB. AsianBondsOnline Data Portal. https://asianbondsonline.adb.org/data-portal/.

Figure 2: Local Currency Bond Issuance Volume in Selected Markets, 2020
(USD billion)

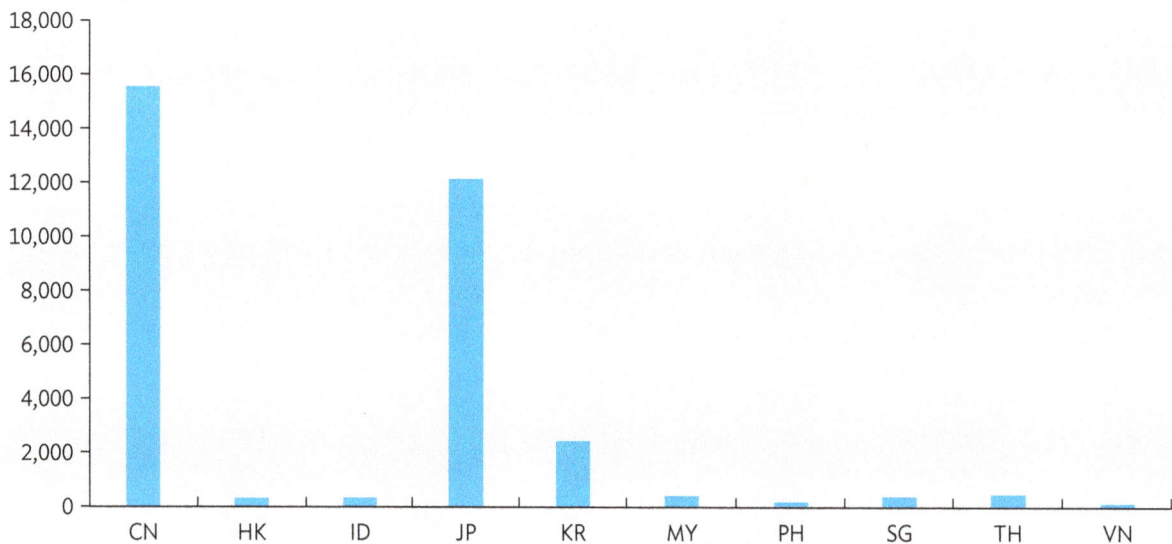

CN = People's Republic of China; HK = Hong Kong, China; ID = Indonesia; JP = Japan; KR = Republic of Korea; MY = Malaysia; PH = Philippines; SG = Singapore; TH = Thailand; USD = United States dollar; VN = Viet Nam.

Source: ADB. AsianBondsOnline Data Portal. https://asianbondsonline.adb.org/data-portal/.

Figure 3: Local Currency Bonds Outstanding as a Share of Gross Domestic Product, 2020
(%)

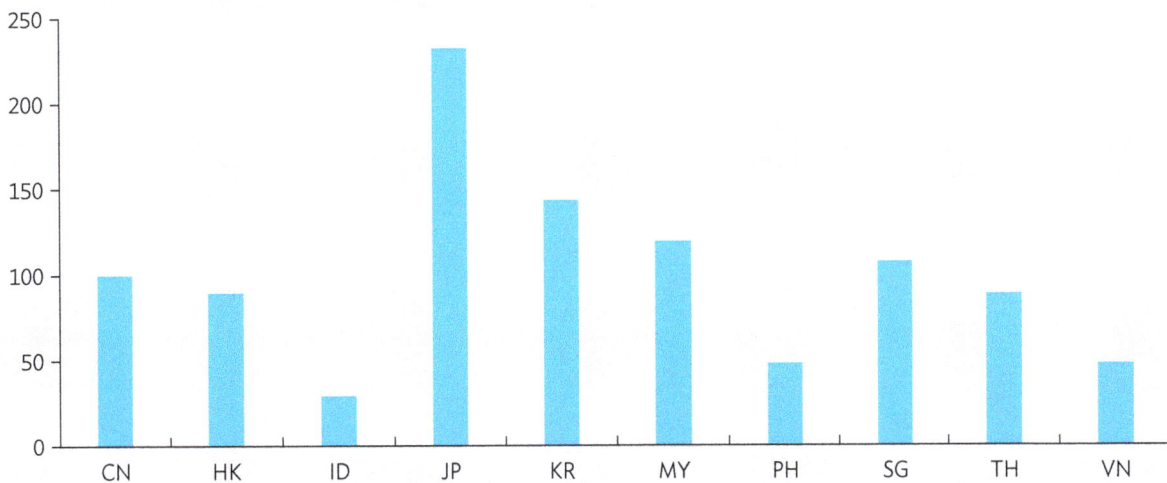

CN = People's Republic of China; HK = Hong Kong, China; ID = Indonesia; JP = Japan; KR = Republic of Korea; MY = Malaysia; PH = Philippines; SG = Singapore; TH = Thailand; VN = Viet Nam.

Source: ADB. AsianBondsOnline Data Portal. https://asianbondsonline.adb.org/data-portal/.

2. Secondary Market

According to the trend of secondary market transactions in the region, fairly notable fluctuations have been witnessed in terms of financial market developments.[3] Transactions surged during the process of responding to the global financial crisis, reaching their highest level in 2011, which was followed by a subsequent decreasing trend until 2017 before rebounding in 2018. The total trading volume of bonds increased 14.1% year-on-year to USD25.6 trillion in 2018, and 35.3% year-on-year to USD34.6 trillion in 2019. The increase in transaction volume since 2017 is largely attributable to the increase in bond issuances (Figure 4).

The bond turnover ratio, which can be calculated by dividing the total turnover of bonds by the stock of bonds outstanding, consequently indicates the utilization of bonds reached a record-high of 2.98 in 2011, decreased to 0.95 in 2017, and then rebounded to 1.28 in 2019. This shows that although the primary bond market in the region is fairly large in size, the secondary market is not yet sufficient. In particular, the amount of bond issuances has increased significantly since 2017, but the trading volume of bonds has not increased that much during the same period, suggesting low turnover ratios in the secondary market.

---

[3] The total size of bond transactions as measured by *AsianBondsOnline* (ABO) includes only outright bond transactions in most regional markets, but not collateral transactions such as repo and derivatives transactions. Consequently, in member economies where repo transactions account for a significant portion of bond transactions, the total volume of collateral transactions is much larger than the amount of general bond transactions provided by ABO.

Figure 4: Bond Trading Volumes and Turnover Ratios
(USD trillion)

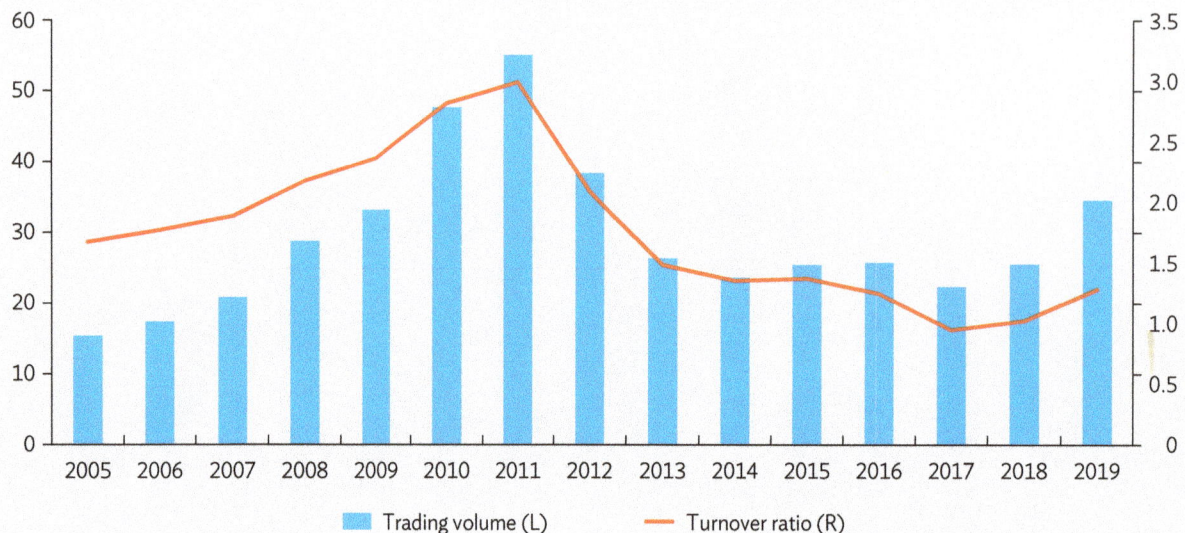

USD = United States dollar.

Source: ADB. AsianBondsOnline Data Portal. https://asianbondsonline.adb.org/data-portal/.

B. Collateral Transactions

The expansion of secured financial transactions can improve market participants' liquidity and reduce their financing costs. Furthermore, it contributes to the promotion of market infrastructure development and the provision of hedging instruments, thereby facilitating the development of LCY bond markets.

In this study, collateral transactions are defined as financial transactions involving bonds as collateral.[4] They include repos, swaps, securities loans, and other over-the-counter derivatives transactions, among which the most actively traded products are repos. Collateral in financial transactions plays an important role in managing counterparty risks, thereby reducing relevant funding costs; for borrowers, for instance, risk-free bonds provided to counterparties can enable them to raise funds at a lower cost. For investors, it can enable them to liquidate bonds held at a minimum loss in the event of a counterparty default, along with the re-hypothecation options.

The region's collateral markets are still in the development phase. Though repo and standing facility, in which government bonds are utilized as collateral, are commonly used in the central banks' monetary operations, government bonds are not traded actively in the secondary market. The use of LCY government bonds for cross-border collateral transactions is still very limited; there may be a few exceptional cases of using Japanese and Chinese government bonds. In recent years, however, collateral transactions have shown a steady increase in the domestic market for some member economies.

---

4   Since this study is aimed at activating the use of LCY bonds for cross-border collateral transactions, only bond collateral was analyzed.

According to collateral transaction data provided by member economies through the survey, the volume of total collateral transactions demonstrates a continuous increase.[5] On a year-on-year basis, it surged 12.3% in 2019 and 22.9% in 2020. Although confined to the case of some member economies,[6] the ratio of collateral transactions to total trading volume of bonds consistently exceeded 80% during the 2018–2020 period.[7] This suggests that collateral transactions of LCY bonds have become more active in the domestic market. Meanwhile, according to the data on the types of collateral transactions, repos explained more than 97% of the total transactions, with other collateral transactions—such as swap, securities lending, and other derivatives—constituting only 2.1%.[8]

However, the picture contains some limitations in the sense that the trading volume of repo transactions in several member economies has not been reported clearly and data for other financial transactions involving collateral—such as swap, securities lending, and other derivatives—have been submitted without clear aggregation in most member economies. Moreover, in the case of cross-border collateral transactions, almost no member economies provided relevant data, which was another dimension of challenge in understanding the volume of transactions. All in all, there were limitations in identifying the complete picture of collateral transactions in the region.

Figure 5: **Trading Volume of Collateral Transaction in ASEAN+3**
(USD trillion, %)

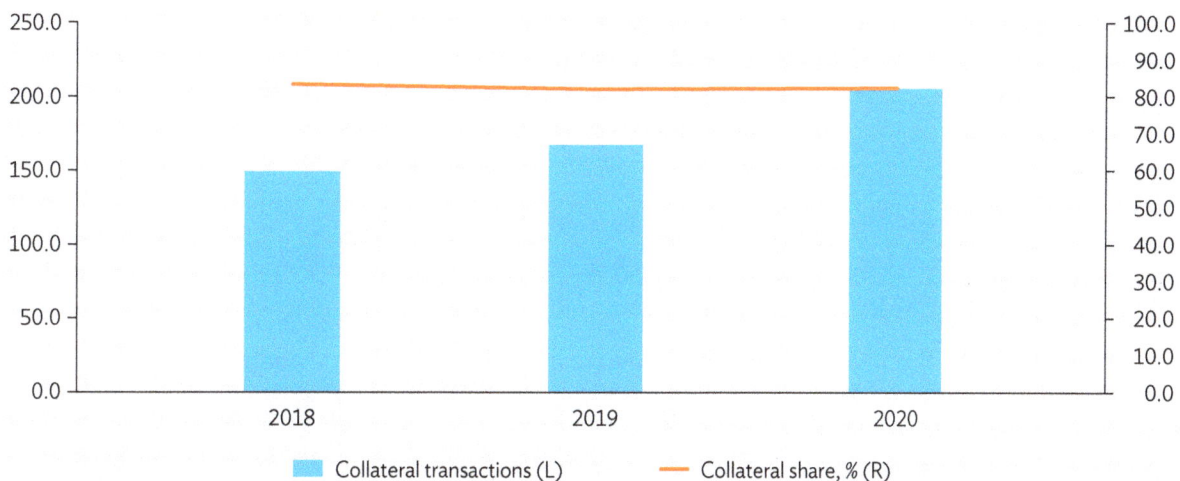

ASEAN+3 = Association of Southeast Asian Nations plus the People's Republic of China, Japan, and the Republic of Korea;
USD = United States dollar.

Note: The total volume of collateral transactions is based on eight economies and the share of collateral transactions is based on five economies.

Source: Cross-Border Settlement Infrastructure Forum Survey (2021).

---

5   Based on eight member economies (the People's Republic of China; Hong Kong, China; the Republic of Korea; Indonesia; Malaysia; the Philippines; Thailand; and Viet Nam) that provided relevant data.

6   Based on five member economies (the People's Republic of China; Hong Kong, China; the Republic of Korea; Malaysia; and Thailand) that provided relevant data.

7   Bond transaction data from ABO and collateral transaction data from each member economy participating in the survey could not be directly compared because the criteria for the compilation of the two statistics differed across economies.

8   Based on the three member economies (the People's Republic of China; the Republic of Korea; and Thailand) that provided relevant data.

Table 2: Trading Volume of Collateral Transactions by Economy
(USD billion)

	2018	2019	2020
Hong Kong, China	2,478.0	3,593.3	3,238.4
Indonesia	14.9	20.1	9.1
Malaysia	26.9	52.6	92.3
People's Republic of China	108,616,6	120,979.0	151,169.1
Philippines	1.9	2.0	0.1
Republic of Korea	29,878.2	34,956.1	41,007.1
Thailand	7,589.7	7,319.4	9,602.5
Viet Nam	0.0	0.0	0.0
Total Collateral Transactions[a]	148,606.3	166,922.5	205,118.5
% of Total Domestic Bond Transactions[b]	83.1	81.8	82.2

USD = United States dollar.

[a] Based on eight economies that provided relevant data.

[b] Based on five economies that provided relevant data.

Source: Cross-Border Settlement Infrastructure Forum Survey (2021).

C. Collateral Eligibility Criteria

1. Collateral Used by Central Banks for Market Operations

The collateral eligibility of central banks is an important indicator in determining the accessibility of financial institutions to central bank liquidity. In general, the eligible collateral of a central bank is based on legal stability, credit requirements, market neutrality, and risk-free assets with large issuances and transactions.

Before the global financial crisis, central banks tended to operate their collateral pools with a narrow scope and with a view to minimizing the possibility of credit loss and achieving market neutrality, thereby immunizing their collateral baskets from price fluctuations and distortions. However, in the process of overcoming the impact of the global financial crisis, central banks expanded the eligibility criteria as a means of stabilizing the market by easing financial institutions' credit and liquidity strains. This decision was to some extent supported by the analytical judgment that the risk of loss could be managed by measures such as the haircut adjustments of individual bonds.

When it comes to the G7 central banks' collateral criteria, the US Federal Reserve had previously operated a relatively narrow range of assets and recognized risk-free assets with active market transactions in order to not affect asset prices. However, in the event of the global financial crisis, the eligibility was greatly expanded to improve the liquidity conditions of financial institutions. In the case of the European Central Bank (ECB), the scope of eligible collateral is relatively wide considering the financial structure of the Eurosystem.

The Bank of England recognizes high-quality bonds such as government bonds and central bank bills as eligible collateral in order to minimize credit and liquidity risks, but also expanded the target collateral to credit securities after the global financial crisis. The Bank of Japan (BOJ) operates relatively wide collateral schemes, recognizing commercial paper and asset-backed commercial paper, along with government bonds.

The survey results showed that central banks in the ASEAN+3 region commonly accept government bonds, central bank bills, and government-guaranteed bonds as eligible collateral. However, in the case of government-guaranteed bonds, requirements of a certain credit rating or higher must be met.

Meanwhile, the number of economies that recognize foreign currency (FCY) assets as eligible collateral is on the rise. Among the member economies, several central banks—including the BOJ, Bank Negara Malaysia (BNM), Bank of Thailand (BOT), Hong Kong Monetary Authority, and Monetary Authority of Singapore (MAS)—acknowledge FCY bonds as collateral. In particular, the parties to cross-border collateral arrangements (CBCAs) accept government bonds and central bank bills of the other parties. However, other member economies still do not recognize FCY bonds as eligible collateral.

Based on the survey results, the following was noted:

(i)　Advanced economies broadly accept securities, including commercial paper, with a certain level of credit rating as collateral. Meanwhile, the eligible collateral in the region is mainly limited to government bonds, central bank bills, and government-guaranteed bonds.

(ii)　Some central banks' collateral includes FCY government bonds and central bank bills, but this is the case only in a few economies in the region.

(iii)　Despite the high quality of government bonds, they are rarely accepted as collateral in global financial markets with the exception of key (or hard) currency bonds such as Japanese Government Bonds.

2. Collateral Used by Market Participants

In the case of general financial market transactions, the eligible collateral pool includes normally all bonds traded in the market without specific restrictions (Table 3). This is because collateral is determined by mutual agreement between the counterparties. However, government bonds and government-guaranteed bonds, which have little credit risk and are also highly liquid, appear to be preferred as collateral.

3. Risk Management

Regional central banks and market participants are applying haircuts and margining arrangements to safeguard them from market and counterparty risks. In other words, only a certain percentage of the mark-to-market value at the time of transaction is recognized as collateral value in view of responding to the fluctuations of the bonds' market prices. An additional haircut is normally applied in the case of FCY bonds to further manage foreign exchange risk when the bonds are accepted as collateral (Table 4).

Table 3: Eligible Collateral Criteria in ASEAN+3

Economy	Central Bank's Repo	OTC Market-Based Repo
Brunei Darussalam	– Government bonds – Central bank bills	NA
People's Republic of China	– Government bonds – Central bank bills, policy bank bonds – High-quality bonds and loans including SMEs, green, and agricultural financial bonds rated AA and above – Corporate credit bonds rated AA and above – Bank-issued perpetual bonds	– All types of bonds
Hong Kong, China	(LCY) – Exchange-fund paper – Government bonds (FCY) – High-quality liquid securities denominated in USD, EUR, RMB, JPY, or GBP, issued by governments or supranationals	– All types of bonds
Indonesia	– Government bonds (including USD-denominated) – Central bank bills – Bonds by other government whose CBs have an agreement with BI	– Government bonds – Central bank bills – Corporate bonds
Japan	(LCY) – Government bonds (FCY) – Government bonds issued by the US, the UK, Germany, or France	– Japanese Government Bonds – Bonds guaranteed by the government – Foreign government bonds – Municipal bonds – Corporate bonds (AA or above)
Republic of Korea	– Government bonds – Central bank bills – Government-guaranteed bonds	– All types of bonds

Malaysia	(LCY) – Government bonds
	        – Central bank bills
	        – Government guaranteed bonds
	        – EMEAP-member governments bonds
	        – Other bonds with AAA-rating
	(FCY) – US Treasury bonds, UK gilts
	        – EMEAP-member governments bonds
	        – Government and/or central bank bonds under CBCA
	        – Other bonds
		– All types of bonds

Philippines	– Government issued debt securities	– Government issued debt securities

Singapore	(LCY) – Singapore government securities
	        – MAS bills
	        – Floating-rate notes
	        – Securities issued by any Singapore Statutory Board
	        – Other bonds with AAA- or AA-rating
	(FCY) – Government and/or central bank bonds under CBCA
		– All types of bonds

Thailand	(LCY) – Government bonds and bills
	        – Central bank bonds and bills
	        – SOE bonds guaranteed by government or with AAA-rating
	(FCY) – Government and/or central bank bonds under CBCA
		– All types of bonds

Viet Nam	– Government bonds – Central bank bills – Government-backed bonds – Local government bonds	– Not specified

ASEAN+3 = Association of Southeast Asian Nations plus the People's Republic of China, Japan, and the Republic of Korea; BI = Bank Indonesia; CB = central bank; CBCA = cross-border collateral arrangement; EMEAP = Executives' Meeting of East Asia-Pacific Central Banks; EUR = euro; FCY = foreign currency; GBP = pound sterling; JPY = Japanese yen; LCY = local currency; MAS = Monetary Authority of Singapore; NA = not applicable; OTC = over-the-counter; RMB = Chinese renminbi; SMEs = small and medium-sized enterprises; SOE = state-owned enterprise; UK = United Kingdom; US = United States; USD = United States dollar.

Sources: Cross-Border Settlement Infrastructure Forum Survey (2021); ADB. *ASEAN+3 Bond Market Guides*.

Table 4: Risk Management

Economy	Central Bank's Repo	OTC Market-Based Repo
Brunei Darussalam	– Haircut	NA
Hong Kong, China	– Discounted market value	NA
Indonesia	– Haircut	– Haircut – Margin call, mark-to-market
Japan	NA	– Haircut, Margin Call (Substitution)
Malaysia	– Haircut – Margin call, mark-to-market	– No prescribed method
People's Republic of China	– Haircut	– Haircut
Philippines	– Haircut	– Haircut – Margin call, mark-to-market
Republic of Korea	– Margin rate	– Haircut – Margin call, mark-to-market
Singapore	– Haircut – Margin call, mark-to-market	NA
Thailand	– Haircut – Margin call, mark-to-market	– Haircut – Margin call, mark-to-market
Viet Nam	– No haircut or margin call (SBV could claim to counterparty)	– Haircut – Margin call, mark-to-market

NA = not applicable, OTC = over-the-counter, SBV = State Bank of Viet Nam.

Sources: Cross-Border Settlement Infrastructure Forum Survey (2021); ADB. *ASEAN+3 Bond Market Guides.*

D. Financial Market Infrastructures

1. Domestic Market Infrastructures

From the survey results, in most regional economies, central securities depositories (CSDs) and real-time gross settlement (RTGS) systems are well in place. In the case of CSDs, central banks operate them directly in several economies. In addition, some economies establish multiple CSDs and operate them separately according to the type of bonds.

Participation of domestic market infrastructures is mostly limited to domestic financial institutions and financial market infrastructures (FMIs). However, some CSDs also allow direct participation of international CSDs (ICSDs).[9] In member economies that do not allow nonresidents to participate directly, foreign investors appoint local custodians or agencies and use local settlement and custody services for LCY bond transactions.

A well-established domestic market infrastructure could be used to link with market infrastructures across the region, thereby efficiently supporting cross-border bond transactions. In this respect, most of the domestic market infrastructures of regional member economies are well equipped (Table 5).

---

[9] An ICSD is a CSD that settles trades in international securities such as Eurobonds, although many also settle trades in various domestic securities, usually through direct or indirect (through local agents) links to local CSDs. Examples of ICSDs include Clearstream, Euroclear, and SIX SIS.

Table 5: ASEAN+3 Domestic Financial Market Infrastructures

Economy	Central Securities Depository			Real-Time Gross Settlement System	
	Operator	Name of System	Government or Corporate Bond	Operator	Name of System
Brunei Darussalam	BDCB	CSD	Government	BDCB	RTGS
Cambodia	CSX	–	Corporate	NBC	RTGS
Hong Kong, China	HKMA	CMU	Both	HKMA	CHATS
Indonesia	BI	BI-SSSS	Government	BI	BI-RTGS
	KSEI	C-BEST	Corporate		
Japan	BOJ	BOJ-NET JGB Services	Government	BOJ	BOJ-NET FTS
	JASDEC	BETS	Corporate		
Republic of Korea	KSD	SSS/e-SAFE	Both	BOK	BOK-Wire+
Lao People's Democratic Republic	–	–	–	BOL	RTGS
Malaysia	BNM	RENTAS-SSDS	Both	BNM	RENTAS-IFTS
People's Republic of China	CCDC	CBGS	Both	PBOC	CIPS2
	CSDC	MNS	Corporate		
	SHCH	SHCH-SSS	Corporate		
Philippines	BTr	BTr-NRoSS	Government	BSP	PhilPaSS[plus]
	PDTC	PDTC	Corporate		
Singapore	MAS	MEPS+ SGS	Government	MAS	MEPS+
	CDP	DCSS	Corporate		
Thailand	TSD	PTI	Both	BOT	BAHTNET
Viet Nam	VSD	VSD-DR system	Both	SBV	IBPS

ASEAN+3 = Association of Southeast Asian Nations plus the People's Republic of China, Japan, and the Republic of Korea; BAHTNET = Bank of Thailand Automated High-Value Transfer Network; BDCB = Brunei Darussalam Central Bank; BETS = Book Entry Transfer Systems; BI = Bank Indonesia; BI-RTGS = Bank Indonesia Real Time Gross Settlement; BI-SSSS = Bank Indonesia-Scripless Securities Settlement System; BNM = Bank Negara Malaysia; BOJ = Bank of Japan; BOJ-NET = Bank of Japan Financial Network System; BOJ-NET FTS = BOJ-NET Funds Transfer System; BOK = Bank of Korea; BOK-Wire+ = Bank of Korea Financial Wire Network; BOL = Bank of the Lao PDR; BOT = Bank of Thailand; BSP = Bangko Sentral ng Pilipinas; BTr = Bureau of the Treasury; BTr-NRoSS = Bureau of the Treasury National Registry of Scripless Securities; C-BEST = Central Depository and Book Entry Settlement System; CBGS = Central Bond General System; CCDC = China Central Depository & Clearing Co., Ltd.; CDP = central depository; CHATS = Clearing House Automated Transfer System; CIPS = cross-border interbank payment system; CMU = Central Moneymarkets Unit; CSD = central securities depository; CSDC = China Securities Depository and Clearing Corporation Limited; CSX = Cambodia Securities Exchange; DCSS = Debt Securities Clearing and Settlement System; e-SAFE = Speedy, Accurate, Faithful, Efficient (KSD's system); HKMA = Hong Kong Monetary Authority; IBPS = interbank electronic payment system; JASDEC = Japan Securities Depository Center, Inc.; JGB = Japanese Government Bond; KSD = Korea Securities Depository; KSEI = Kustodian Sentral Efek Indonesia (Indonesia Central Securities Depository); MAS = Monetary Authority of Singapore; MEPS+ = MAS Electronic Payment System; MNS = Multilateral Net Settlement System; NBC = National Bank of Cambodia; PBOC = People's Bank of China; PDTC = Philippine Depository & Trust Corp.; PhilPaSS[plus] = Philippine Payment and Settlement System; PTI = Post Trade Integration; RENTAS-IFTS = Real-Time Electronic Transfer of Funds and Securities–Interbank Funds Transfer System; RENTAS-SSDS = Real-Time Electronic Transfer of Funds and Securities–Scripless Securities Depository and Settlement System; RTGS = Real Time Gross Settlement; SBV = State Bank of Vietnam; SHCH = Shanghai Clearing House; SSS = Securities Settlement System; TSD = Thailand Securities Depository; VSD = Viet Nam Securities Depository; VSD-DR system = Vietnam Securities Depository-Depository Registration system.

Sources: Cross-Border Settlement Infrastructure Forum Survey (2021); ADB. *ASEAN+3 Bond Market Guides.*

2. Linkages between Market Infrastructures

To support cross-border collateral transactions, linkages between market infrastructures are desirable to execute transactions spontaneously. While domestic market infrastructures have been put in place, there are limited cases of linkages in place for cross-border clearing and settlement. As Table 6 indicates, some member economies operate the arrangement by linking their domestic CSDs to foreign RTGSs, CSDs, or ICSDs to support nonresidents' LCY bond transactions. CSIF has discussed this issue for a considerable time and published several reports.

a. CSD–RTGS Linkage

The linkage between CSD and RTGS enables LCY bonds to be settled delivery-versus-payment (DVP) via central bank money, which ensures the safety of the settlement, even in cross-border transactions. This linkage could facilitate further banking and financial integration in the ASEAN+3 region. Furthermore, CSD–RTGS linkage can not only support risk mitigation by enabling cross-currency DVP and mobilizing LCY bonds, but it can also facilitate cross-currency agreements, and therefore alleviate concerns of collateral shortage.[10]

The linkage between the Bank of Japan Financial Network System–Japanese Government Bond Services (BOJ-NET JGB Services) and the Hong Kong Clearing House Automated Transfer System is an example of CSD–RTGS linkage (Figure 6). The link, which can enable DVP settlement of Japanese Government Bonds and Hong Kong dollars, launched in April 2021.

Figure 6: Linkage between Bank of Japan Financial Network System–Japanese Government Bonds Services and Hong Kong Clearing House Automated Transfer System

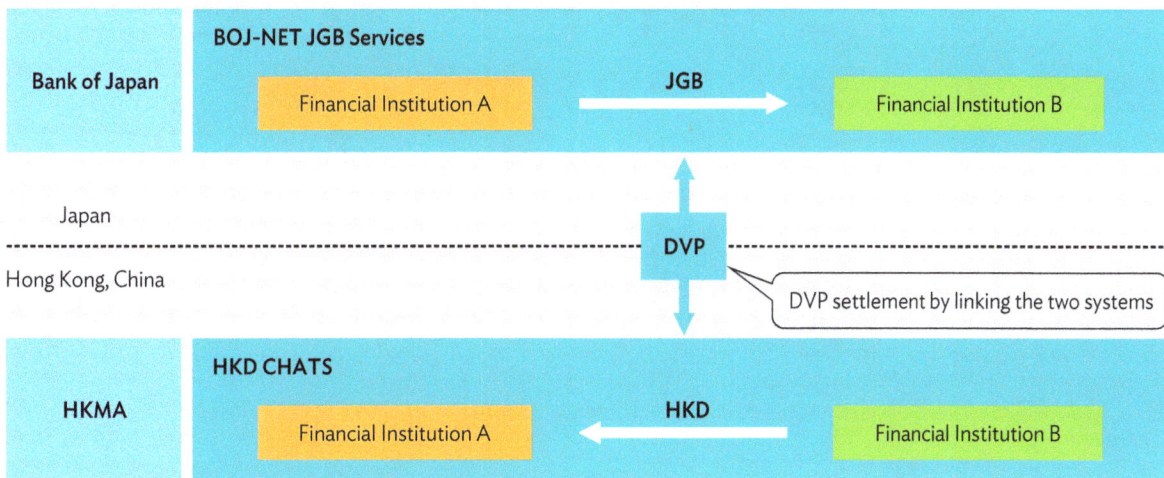

BOJ-NET = Bank of Japan Financial Network System, CHATS = Clearing House Automated Transfer System, DVP = delivery-versus-payment, HKD = Hong Kong dollar, HKMA = Hong Kong Monetary Authority, JGB = Japanese Government Bond.
Source: ADB. 2020. *Next Steps for ASEAN+3 Central Securities Depository and Real-Time Gross Settlement Linkages: A Progress Report of the Cross-Border Settlement Infrastructure Forum.*

[10] For more detail, see ADB. 2020. *Next Steps for ASEAN+3 Central Securities Depository and Real-Time Gross Settlement Linkages: A Progress Report of the Cross-Border Settlement Infrastructure Forum,* pp. 14–16.

Through this linkage, Japanese financial institutions operating in the financial market of Hong Kong, China could directly finance the Hong Kong dollar via repurchase agreements secured by Japanese Government Bonds held in their home country.

b. CSD–CSD Linkage

Another case is the linkage between regional CSDs with each other. It includes the link between China Central Depository & Clearing Co., Ltd. (CCDC) and Shanghai Clearing House Co., Ltd. of the People's Republic of China and the Central Moneymarkets Unit of Hong Kong, China (Figure 7).[11]

Figure 7: Linkage between China Central Depository & Clearing Co., Ltd. and Shanghai Clearing House of the People's Republic of China, and Central Moneymarkets Unit of Hong Kong, China

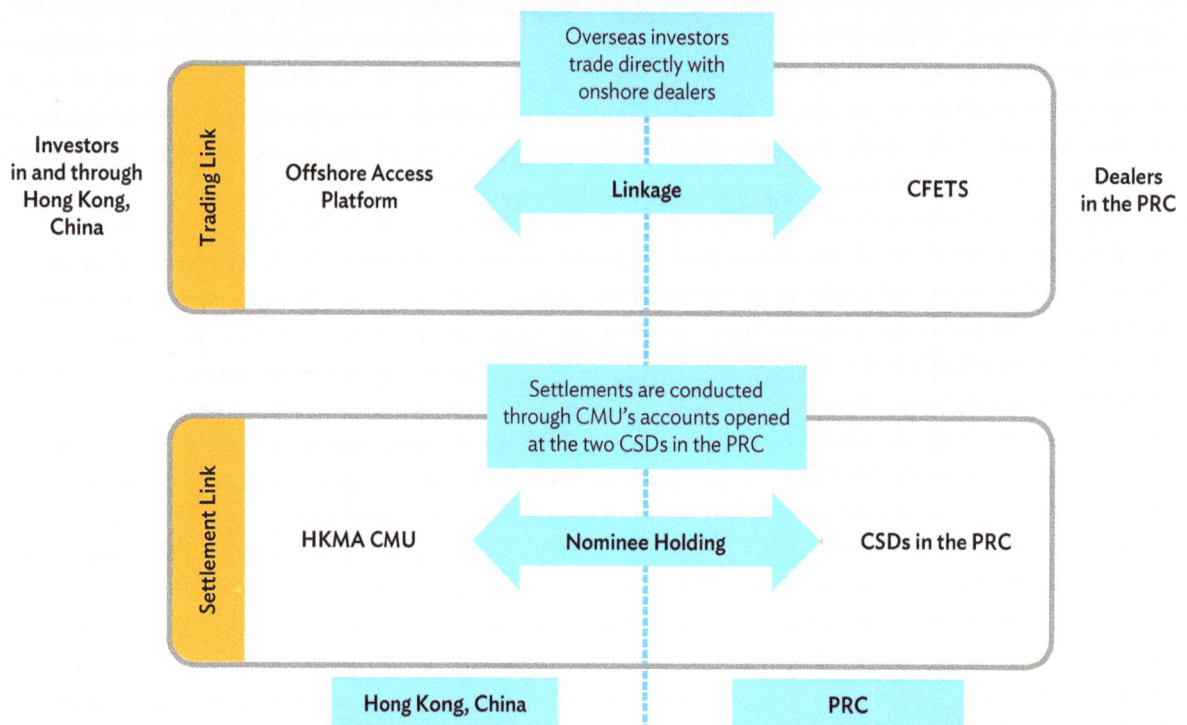

CFETS = China Foreign Exchange Trade System, CMU = Central Moneymarkets Unit, CSD = central securities depository, HKMA = Hong Kong Monetary Authority, PRC = People's Republic of China.

Source: ADB. 2020. *Next Steps for ASEAN+3 Central Securities Depository and Real-Time Gross Settlement Linkages: A Progress Report of the Cross-Border Settlement Infrastructure Forum.*

---

[11]   Footnote 10, p. 17.

Meanwhile, international linkages exist in regional markets with nonresident participation. Foreign investors use domestic CSDs for LCY bond transactions in local markets. To this end, many foreign investors use ICSDs' services or local custodian services to avoid the cost of developing financial market infrastructures. Therefore, some member economies have linked their CSDs to ICSDs or have a plan to link in the future to support foreign investors (Table 6).

Table 6: **Cross-Border Linkages between Market Infrastructures**

	Linkages
People's Republic of China	CBGS, SHCH-SSS – HKMA CMU, Euroclear
Hong Kong, China	HKMA CMU – CBGS, SHCH-SSS, HKMA CHATS – BOJ-NET JGBs
Indonesia	BI-SSSS – Clearstream
Japan	BOJ-NET JGBs – HKMA CHATS
Republic of Korea	e-SAFE – Euroclear, Clearstream
Malaysia	RENTAS-SSDS – Euroclear
Thailand	PTI – Plan to Connect with Global Custodian

BI-SSSS = Bank Indonesia-Scripless Securities Settlement System; BOJ-NET JGBs = Bank of Japan Financial Network System Japanese Government Bond Service; CBGS = Central Bond General System; e-SAFE = Speedy, Accurate, Faithful, Efficient (KSD's system); HKMA CHATS = Hong Kong Monetary Authority Clearing House Automated Transfer System; HKMA CMU = Hong Kong Monetary Authority Central Moneymarkets Unit; PTI = Post Trade Integration; RENTAS-SSDS = Real-Time Electronic Transfer of Funds and Securities - Scripless Securities Depository and Settlement System; SHCH-SSS = Shanghai Clearing House Securities Settlement System.

Source: Cross-Border Settlement Infrastructure Forum Survey (2021).

III

CROSS-BORDER COLLATERAL ARRANGEMENTS

A. Basic Concept of a Cross-Border Collateral Arrangement

A cross-border collateral arrangement (CBCA) is a monetary policy instrument in which the central banks of the two countries enter into a reciprocal arrangement to provide liquidity to domestic financial institutions accepting FCY bonds as collateral. In other words, CBCA is a policy tool that helps the central bank smoothly supply its liquidity to foreign financial institutions operating in its market with FCY bonds held in their home countries.

If CBCAs become more widely available in the region, a series of benefits might be expected, such as increased liquidity in the financial markets, more developed LCY bond markets, and an expanded regional financial safety net:

- CBCAs are likely to increase the liquidity of financial institutions as a central bank's eligible collateral pool becomes wider.
- From the emerging markets perspective, CBCAs could help the development of their domestic financial markets by providing tools for accessing LCY liquidity to global financial institutions and contributing to expanding operations in their markets.
- It could increase the cross-border usage of high-quality bonds such as government bonds, which are denominated in local currencies.
- It could also lay the foundation for supporting mutual entrance of financial institutions across the region along with facilitating Qualified ASEAN Banks (QABs).
- Above all, CBCAs could reduce adverse systemic impacts by allowing market participants to address liquidity shortages and contribute to expanding the financial safety net and strengthening the financial stability in the region.

As a result, CBCAs could be the effective way to enhance cross-border collateral transactions between LCY bond markets.

Notwithstanding the potential benefits, there are some issues to consider in promoting CBCAs:

- From the central bank's perspective, the typical structure of CBCA in which the central bank bears risks related to collateral value and currency mismatch could make it difficult to enter into an arrangement.

- Cross-border collateral transactions may lead to varying degrees of legal uncertainties stemming from significant differences in laws and regulatory frameworks across jurisdictions in the region.

- Due to the gaps in sovereign credit ratings between developed and developing economies, as well as the differences in international business activities of financial institutions, the effect of CBCAs in developing markets may be limited. In the case of emerging markets, for instance, it would be harder to utilize the CBCA on a mutual basis as it is more likely that their LCY-denominated assets are not recognized as eligible collateral by their advanced economy counterparts.

- Local liquidity funding costs may increase if the margin rate is too high to reflect foreign exchange risk and differences of bond credit ratings in the region, where the currencies used are all different and the credit ratings of bonds varies. In fact, some central banks have added a certain ratio to the margin rate applied to their currency bonds when accepting FCY-denominated bonds as collateral.

- The potential benefits of CBCAs may be somewhat limited at a time when financial institutions are not actively operating in overseas markets.

Consequently, the introduction of CBCAs is influenced by the central bank's monetary policy, the collateral capacity of financial institutions, and market infrastructures. Therefore, central banks that provide liquidity need to consider in-depth the impact of the use of CBCA on financial institutions' liquidity management, cost–benefit analysis, and domestic market infrastructures.

Besides CBCA, there are various schemes in which central banks can provide liquidity to financial institutions such as central bank currency swap (CBCS). However, CBCA and CBCS are different in terms of policy target, collateral, and policy implementation mechanism (see Box: Central Bank Currency Swap).

B. Potential Implementation Models

CBCAs currently have several models that have been applied or presented.[12] CBCAs can be divided into two groups, depending on how much the central bank is engaged and where collateral is located. The first group is the correspondent central banking model (CCBM), and the second group is the non-CCBM (see Appendix 1 for more detail).

A central bank can decide the most appropriate CBCA model to tackle its own needs and constraints. After all, the most important factor in choosing the CBCA model is the involvement of the central bank. It is also an important consideration of how to manage the risk of FCY-denominated collateral.

1. Correspondent Central Banking Model

The CCBM is a method in which the central bank of the country where the collateral is located acts as a custodian bank if the whereabouts of bonds used as collateral and liquidity actually supplied are different. The CCBM can be divided back into four types—standard CCBM, CCBM with links, tri-party CCBM, and guarantee CCBM—depending on the type of collateral management services.[13]

---

[12]   Each model is described in detail in Appendix 1.

[13]   For each correspondent central banking model, see European Central Bank (ECB). 2022. *Correspondent central banking model (CCBM) Procedures for Eurosystem Counterparties.* Frankfurt; and Bank for International Settlements (BIS). 2006. *Cross-border collateral arrangements.* Basel, pp. 21–27.

Box: Central Bank Currency Swap

Both central bank currency swaps (CBCSs) and central bank collateral arrangements (CBCAs) are typical monetary policy instruments in which the central banks of two economies enter into mutual arrangements to supply liquidity to financial institutions.

A CBCS allows central banks to provide foreign currency liquidity to the domestic commercial banks in their jurisdictions (box figure). On the other hand, a CBCA allows central banks to provide local currency liquidity to the commercial bank foreign branches in their jurisdictions (Figure 8).

Both policy instruments could contribute to financial stability by allowing central banks to supply liquidity to financial institutions that lack such. However, a notable difference between the two instruments is that CBCS supplies foreign currencies such as major currencies to the domestic financial institutions, while CBCA supplies local currencies to local branches of foreign financial institutions. Therefore, the two policy instruments differ greatly in terms of policy targets and implementation mechanism.

Table: Comparison of Central Bank Currency Swap and Central Bank Collateral Arrangement

	Central Bank Currency Swap	Central Bank Collateral Arrangement
Implementation Body	– Central bank	– Central bank
Policy Targets	– Domestic financial institutions	– Foreign financial institution local branches
Collateral	– Central bank to central bank: local currency – Central bank to financial institution: local currency or foreign currency bonds	– Local currency bonds
Policy Objectives	– Strengthening financial stability – Enhancing financial cooperation between economies – Promoting the internationalization of local currency	– Strengthening financial stability – Facilitating the use of local currency bonds for cross-border financial transactions

Source: Authors' compilation.

Figure: Central Bank Currency Swap

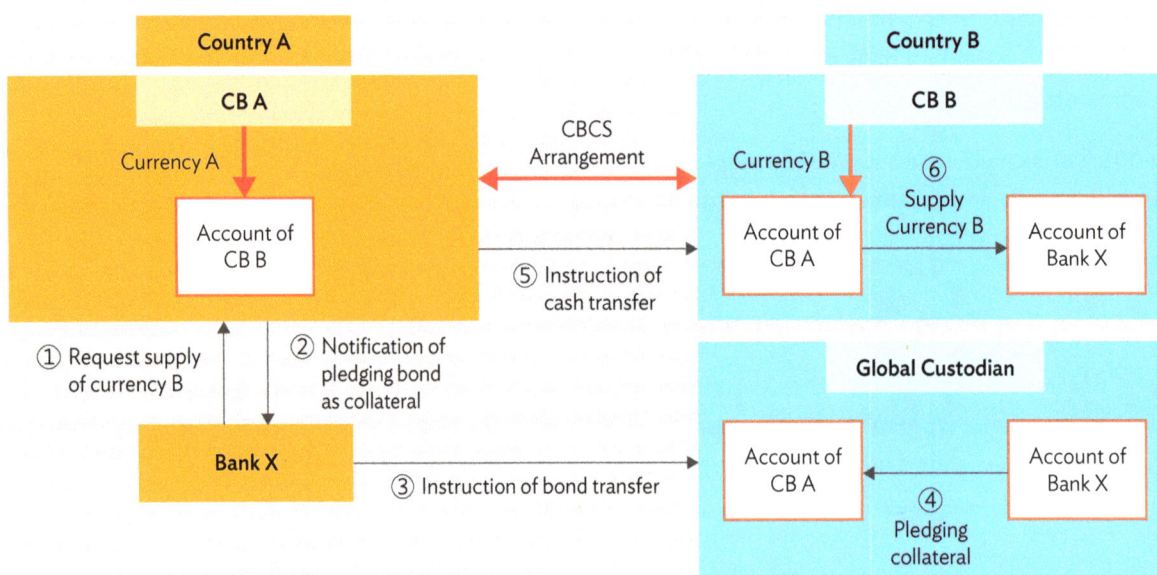

CB = central bank, CBCS = central bank currency swap.
Source: Authors' compilation.

Among the CCBMs, the standard CCBM is simple and realistic compared to other models, considering the structure and the burden of central banks. This model also has the advantage of additional investment not being necessary because it relies primarily on existing market infrastructures. Therefore, in the euro area, the standard CCBM accounts for more than half of the total cases witnessed.

- **Standard CCBM.** Under this model, the correspondent central bank (CCB) acts as a custodian for the home central bank (HCB), which accepts the collateral located in its local securities settlement system (SSS) from the counterparty. Based on the collateral pledged at the CCB, the HCB provides LCY liquidity to its domestic counterparty (Figure 8).

- **CCBM with links.** This model has the same basic structure as the standard CCBM and is mainly utilized when the issuing and holding institutions of the collateral are different. The two countries' SSSs can be very useful when they are interconnected (Appendix 1, Figure A1.2).

- **Tri-Party CCBM.** Under this model, the HCB and its counterparties rely on a collateral management service (CMS). The CMS can take the form of a tripartite collateral service operated by an SSS or a custodian. This model provides a basis for the cross-border use of tri-party collateral management services, whereby the CCB of a market where tri-party collateral management services are being offered for cross-border use acts as a custodian for the HCB with local counterparties wishing to take advantage of such services on a cross-border basis (Appendix 1, Figure A1.3).

- **Guarantee CCBM.** Under this model, the CCB acts as a guarantor for the HCB with respect to assets pledged in its local depository or SSS. Importantly, the instrument backing this arrangement is a guarantee from the CCB on the value of collateral received (Appendix 1, Figure A1.4).

Figure 8: Standard Correspondent Central Banking Model

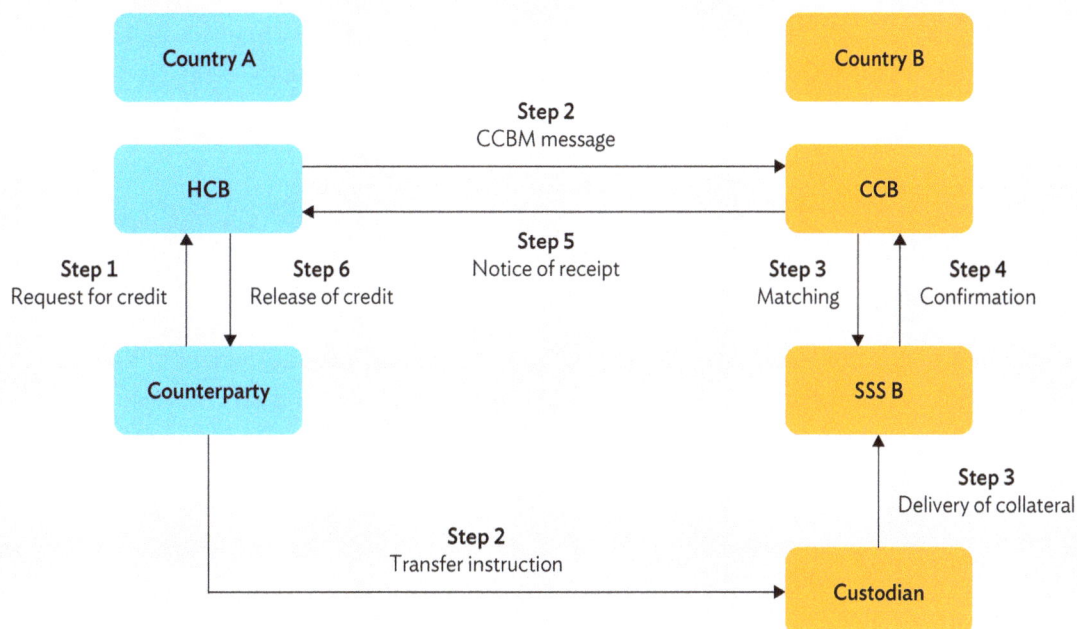

CCB = correspondent central bank, CCBM = correspondent central banking model, HCB = home central bank, SSS B = securities settlement system in Country B.

Source: European Central Bank. 2019. *Correspondent Central Banking Model Procedures for Eurosystem Counterparties.* Frankfurt.

In the ASEAN+3 region, CCBMs that require the role of central banks of both economies will be appropriate because the currencies used vary across regional economies and the degree of market integration is still insufficient.

2. Non-Correspondent Central Banking Model

Non-CCBM could be utilized when the central bank of the lender (HCB) receives collateral directly using its market infrastructures and supplies liquidity based on that action regardless of the collateral-based country's central bank. This is not a CCBM method, so it does not receive correspondent central banking business support from central banks in areas where collateral is located. This includes direct links, relayed links, and remote access.[14]

- **Direct links.** In this model, CSDs in both countries directly link the securities settlement systems (SSSs) without intermediaries to transfer collateral from the issuing institution to the investment institution (counterparty) and receive it as collateral by the HCB (Appendix 1, Figure A1.5).

- **Relayed links.** This model is used when a multiparty CSD linked to the SSS transfers collateral from the secured securities issuer to the investment institution via an intermediary and receives it as collateral by the HCB. It is a contractual and technical arrangement for the transfer of secured securities involving at least three SSSs: the "investor" SSS, the "issuer" SSS, and the "intermediary" SSS (Appendix 1, Figure A1.6).

- **Remote access.** Under this model, both the HCB and its counterparty directly access a foreign-located SSS in which the collateral is available. The HCB accepts the collateral from its counterparty via the foreign-located SSS. This model relies on the existing market infrastructure but requires that the HCB acquire significant knowledge about the functioning of foreign SSSs. Therefore, it may imply additional operational costs for the HCB (Appendix 1, Figure A1.7).

These three models are available between euro area countries, where financial markets are fully integrated and a single currency is used. Consequently, it is difficult to introduce them in the ASEAN+3 region.

C. Existing Models of Cross-Border Collateral Arrangement

1. Euro Area Case

National central banks in the euro area provide liquidity to their foreign financial institutions by accepting euro bonds issued outside of their countries as well as FCY-denominated bonds as collateral. Financial institutions in the euro area are using four models of CBCA—standard CCBM, CCBM with links, direct links, and relayed links—to fund LCY liquidity (Figure 9).

Among these models, the standard CCBM accounts for more than half of the total cases witnessed, followed by the direct links model with 24% (Figure 10).

---

[14] For each non-correspondent central banking model, see ECB. List of Eligible Links. Frankfurt. https://www.ecb.europa.eu/paym/coll/coll/ssslinks/; and BIS. 2006. *Cross-border collateral arrangements*. Basel, pp. 21–27.

**Figure 9: Collateral Mobilized via the Correspondent Central Banking Model
and Eligible Links in the Euro Area**
(EUR billion)

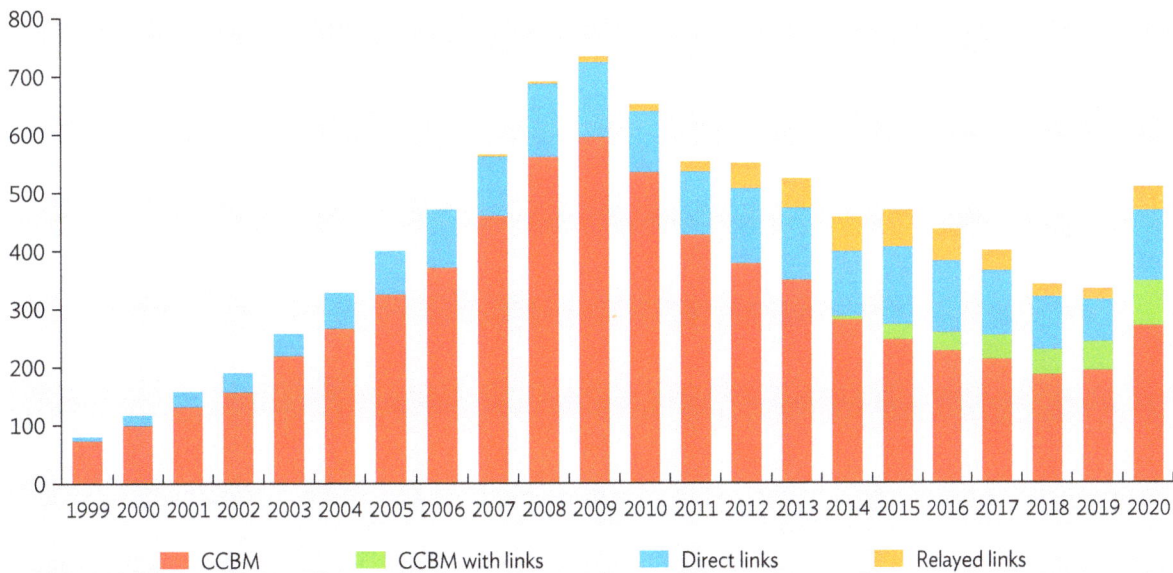

CCBM = correspondent central banking model, EUR = euro.
Source: European Central Bank. *Evolution of Collateral Mobilized via the CCBM and Eligible Links.* Frankfurt. https://www.ecb.europa.eu/stats/.

**Figure 10: Composition Ratio by Cross-Border Collateral Arrangement Models
of the European Central Bank in 2020**

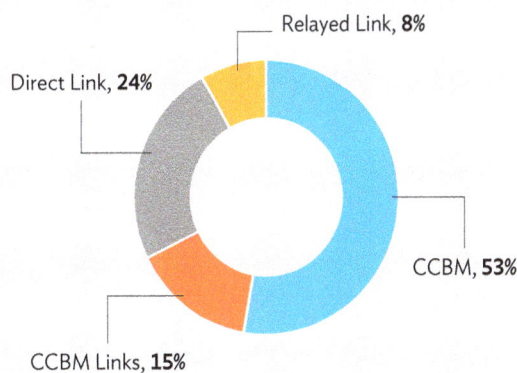

CCBM = correspondent central banking model.
Source: European Central Bank. *Evolution of Collateral Mobilized via the CCBM and Eligible Links.* Frankfurt. https://www.ecb.europa.eu/stats/.

Using these CBCA models, national central banks in the euro area are establishing collateral-based liquidity facilities while overcoming the restriction that mandates limiting of the collateral to the locations. This is also to ensure consistency in the management of collateral. The ECB sets common collateral eligibility. Eligible collateral includes bonds issued in US dollar, pound sterling, and Japanese yen in addition to euro bonds. Cross-border usage of LCY bonds may be an effective policy measure to mitigate collateral shortage.

The key rationale explaining CBCAs that are prevalent in the euro area is as follows:

- The currency is unified into the euro, eliminating the foreign exchange risk.
- It is very easy to mobilize foreign collateral through linking not only the member countries' payment systems, but also the SSSs. The ECB operates the Target 2 system, which integrates the payment system of each member country; and developed the Target 2 Securities platform, which integrates the SSS between members. Through these integrated market infrastructures, even if collateral is located outside of the country, it is easy to accept and verify collateral and provide local liquidity.

On the other hand, other than the euro area, central banks in the US, the United Kingdom, Switzerland, and Sweden, for example, have already introduced CBCAs and are primarily using the standard CCBM to accept FCY collateral. In particular, bonds denominated in euros and other foreign currencies are widely accepted as collateral.[15]

2. ASEAN+3 Case

A few central banks in the region have signed CBCAs that accept FCY bonds. The Bank of Japan (BOJ) has signed CBCAs with three central banks: Bank Indonesia, the Bank of Thailand (BOT), and the Monetary Authority of Singapore (MAS).[16] Under these CBCAs, the central banks of the other economies only accept Japanese Government Bonds as collateral and provide local liquidity to their foreign financial institutions, while the BOJ does not accept collateral from the other economies (Figure 11).

Figure 11: Cross-Border Collateral Arrangement Model of the Bank of Japan

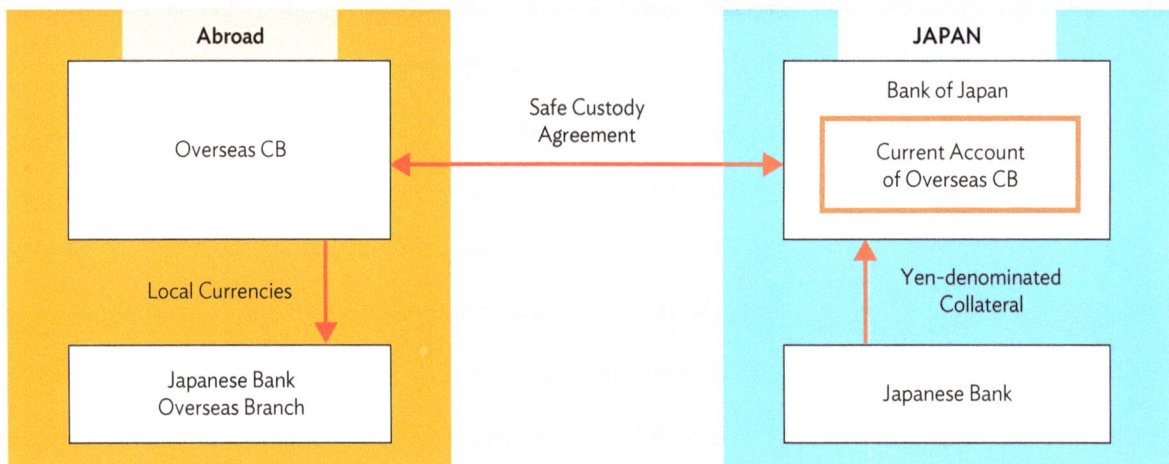

CB = central bank.
Source: Cross-Border Settlement Infrastructure Forum Survey (2021).

---

[15]   It includes euro, US dollar, pound sterling, Japanese yen, Danish krona, Swedish krona, and Norwegian krona.

[16]   There is a liquidity supply arrangement between the BOJ and the Bangko Sentral ng Pilipinas (BSP). It is a cross-border liquidity arrangement (CBLA), but is secured with Japanese yen (cash collateral) rather than bonds. In addition to the CBCA with regional central banks, the BOJ has also signed collateral arrangements with the central banks of the US, the United Kingdom, Germany, and France, and is accepting government bonds from these countries as collateral.

In addition, three central banks—the Bank Negara Malaysia (BNM), BOT, and MAS—have signed bilateral CBCAs with each other.[17] They use the standard CCBM to implement arrangements. However, it is observed that the CBCAs in the ASEAN+3 region adopted by central banks are the ones implemented only in emergency situations. This is mainly because such arrangements have been established as one of the central bank monetary policies to respond to the global financial turmoil. As a result, these were rarely executed in normal times. The arrangement among the central banks is to accept central bank bills in addition to government bonds as collateral. Meanwhile, the arrangement between the BOT and the MAS related to the eligible collateral remains a work in progress (Figure 12).

In the survey responses, central banks that currently do not have a CBCA indicated the standard CCBM as the most likely model for use, should they need to consider the measure of availability and ease of implementation based on incumbent market infrastructures.

Figure 12: **Cross-Border Collateral Arrangement Model of the Monetary Authority of Singapore**

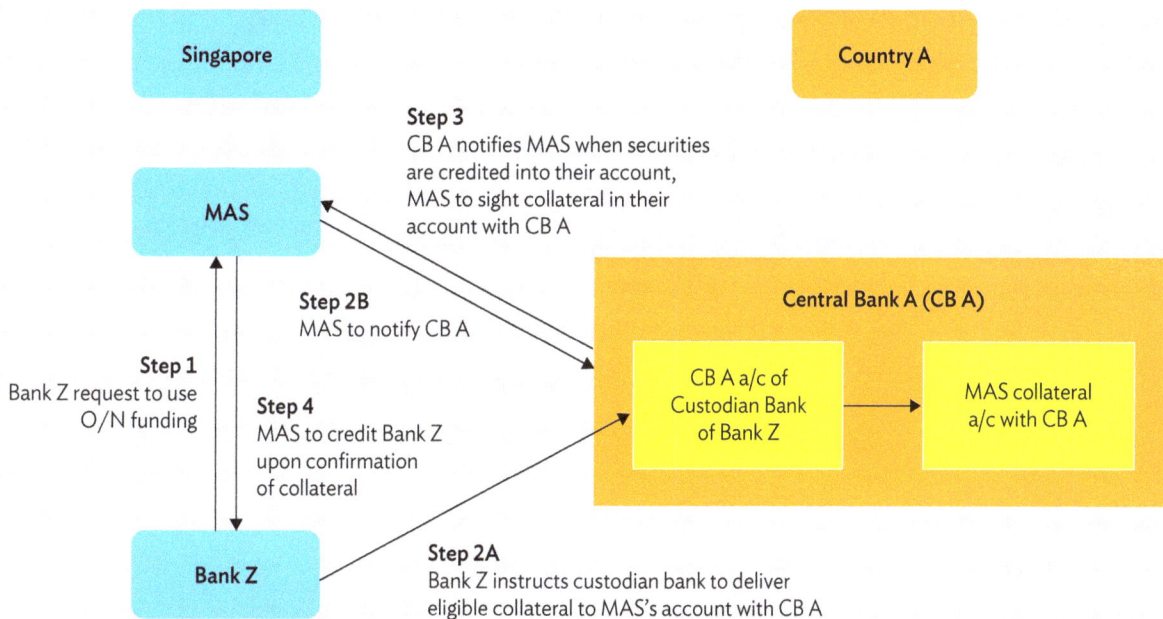

CB A = central bank A, MAS = Monetary Authority of Singapore.
Source: Cross-Border Settlement Infrastructure Forum Survey (2021).

[17] In addition to the regional central banks, the MAS also signed CBCAs with central banks of the US, the United Kingdom, Germany, France, and the Netherlands.

IV

THE USE OF LOCAL CURRENCY BONDS AS CROSS-BORDER COLLATERAL

A. Overview of Cross-Border Collateral Transactions

Although collateral transactions in the region have been on the rise since the global financial crisis, the vast majority of cross-border transactions are limited to major currencies. The use of LCY bonds as collateral can play a critical role in preventing market malfunctions due to external shocks. It also allows better and swift risk management and the expansion of market liquidity. In addition, flexible use of domestic bonds for cross-border collateral transactions supports the development of LCY bond markets, diversifies financial instruments, and expands bonds' mobility to respond to strengthening global financial regulations.

The survey results showed that collateral transactions are mainly undertaken within domestic markets and rarely cross borders. In addition, many regional central banks recognize bonds based mainly on their own currencies as eligible assets. Only a few central banks—including the BNM, BOJ, BOT, Hong Kong Monetary Authority, and MAS—accept FCY assets as collateral (Table 3). Therefore, discussions on bond market development strategies are needed along with the expansion of eligible collateral pools. In particular, since collateral is at the heart of risk management and securities financing, it is necessary to analyze factors that affect collateral demand.

B. Key Factors Influencing Collateral Demand

The factors affecting the demand for collateral vary widely due to the diversity and complexity of financial transactions. Looking at the demand factors, first, the central bank's collateral policy can be identified as an important element. Next, changes in market participants' perceptions, integrations, or linkages of global financial markets and tightened financial regulations following the global financial crisis may affect the demand for collateral.

1. Central Bank Collateral Policy

After the global financial crisis, the impact on central bank collateral policies has increased. As shown in Figure 13, the Bank for International Settlements (BIS) viewed the "secondary market liquidity (tradability)" as the biggest factor that affects the demand for collateral, followed by the "central bank operating frameworks"

Figure 13: Factors Influencing Participation in Collateral Markets
(% of respondents identifying the factor as important)

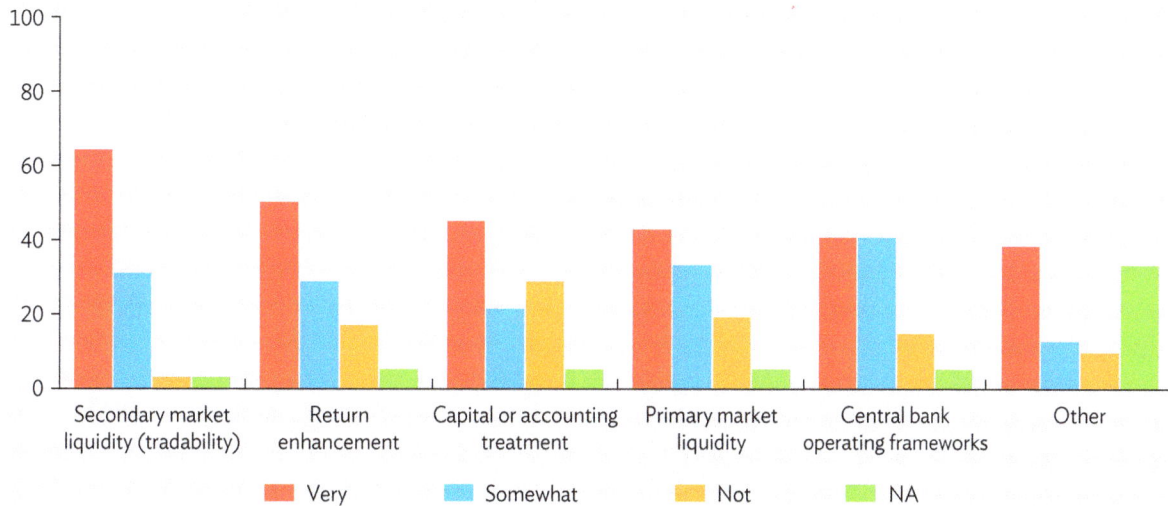

NA = not applicable.

Source: Bank for International Settlements. 2015. *Central Bank Operating Frameworks and Collateral Markets*. Basel.

as a major factor.[18] A central bank's liquidity policy and subsequent collateral policy have a significant impact on the risk management of the private sector. For example, in the process of overcoming the global financial crisis, central banks around the world have greatly expanded the collateral eligibility to provide liquidity to financial institutions, which in turn has affected the activation of collateral transactions.

The expansion of the scope of eligible collateral could reduce the possibility of restrictions on transactions between financial institutions and central banks. Financial institutions with a large number of eligible bonds could improve their financing capacity. Central banks also signed CBCAs separately from currency swaps to expand liquidity to financial institutions (Figure 13).

2. Changes in Market Participants' Perceptions

Counterparty risk management has been emphasized since the global financial crisis. The recognition of collateral needs has significantly increased since then. A high level of recognition by market participants is an important factor affecting collateral demand. Market participants became more mindful of the risk of unsecured financial transactions. Since capital surcharges are becoming more critical and burdensome to banking, the use of collateral to reduce risk weight seems an inevitable option.

It is becoming more important to use appropriate collateral for secured financial transactions. The identification and utilization of appropriate collateral in cross-border transactions is also recognized as an important factor in financial stability. However, the development of LCY bond markets has yet to be linked to the momentum in the region due to market constraints and policy measures.

[18] BIS. 2015. *Central Bank Operating Frameworks and Collateral Markets*. Basel.

3. Integration and Linkages of Global Financial Markets

Global financial markets have become increasingly integrated and financial activities have been expanding across countries. Globalization of financial markets is also underway due to more linkages between market infrastructures. In particular, ASEAN is pushing for the integration of financial markets by introducing QABs, which is part of the agenda of the ASEAN Banking Integration Framework (ABIF). These environments have given market participants the challenge of managing multiple currencies' liquidity. However, market participants' risk management capabilities are hindered primarily by the limitations of existing financial market infrastructures designed to meet the needs of domestic transactions.

In an environment where financial markets are integrated and financial market infrastructures are interconnected, the activation of cross-border collateral transactions eventually affects the demand for collateral.

4. Strengthening Global Financial Regulations

Even though non-internationally active financial institutions are minimally affected by the extensive global financial regulatory reforms, those movements have led to changes in risk management practices of financial institutions, which inevitably affects the demand for high-quality liquid assets (HQLA).[19] For example, the Basel III liquidity coverage ratio and BIS-IOSCO requirements for non-cleared derivatives are directly contributing to the increase in demand for HQLA.[20] Failure to secure high-quality eligible collateral may result in liquidity difficulties due to increased financing costs.

In addition, the mandate of standardized over-the-counter (OTC) derivatives to clear up the central clearing counterparty (CCP) from OTC transactions not only increases market participants' demand for initial margin but also increases the frequency of collateral being pledged for variation margin.[21] In other words, in the financial market, the implementation of the mandatory margin system for OTC derivatives has an impact on market participants. As such, the measure of Basel III and non-clearing derivatives are factors that increase the demand for high-quality assets.

The capability to secure liquidity in the market is being recognized as a key financial capacity. However, there is a limit to responding to changes in the global environment as the liquidity market using collateral in the region has not been developed that much.

---

[19]   Assets are considered to be HQLA if they can be easily and immediately converted into cash at little or no loss of value. BIS. 2013. *Basel III: The Liquidity Coverage Ratio and Liquidity Risk Monitoring Tools*. Basel.

[20]   The liquidity coverage ratio aims to ensure that a bank has an adequate stock of unencumbered HQLA, which consist of cash or assets that can be converted into cash at little or no loss of value in private markets to meet its liquidity needs for a 30-calendar-day liquidity stress scenario. BIS. 2013. *Basel III: The Liquidity Coverage Ratio and Liquidity Risk Monitoring Tools*. Basel.

[21]   In 2009, the G20 leaders agreed to reforms in the OTC derivatives market to achieve central clearing and, where appropriate, exchange or electronic trading of standardized OTC derivatives; the reporting of all transactions to trade repositories; and higher capital as well as margin requirements for non-centrally cleared transactions.

C. Potential Benefits

If cross-border collateral transactions become available, financial transactions using LCY-denominated bonds will also be active. In addition, market participants' more effective risk management and their financial cost reduction might be possible as the importance of collateral is highlighted. Furthermore, the vitalization of collateral transactions across the region could expand market liquidity and contribute to regional financial stability.

1. Contribution to Financial Stability

It is important to note that some Asian LCY government bonds are now rated as highly as the government bonds of major markets. In addition, the liquidity of Asian government bonds may be much higher than highly rated USD-denominated corporate bonds. To determine the value of collateral, it is necessary to consider not only credit ratings but also liquidity. In other words, modest-quality but highly liquid assets may be more usable as collateral than high-quality but illiquid assets because credit quality can be adjusted by haircuts. By expanding eligibility of collateral to Asian government bonds in a more flexible manner, it will not only improve flexibility in risk management but also increase resilience at the time of operational difficulty arising from market disruption because central banks will provide liquidity through their market operations at times of stress. Moreover, the use of cross-border collateral in the region can have a greater positive effect as the liquidation of collateral can take place without a concern related to time differences.

By making more active and flexible CBCA, the central bank can provide rapid liquidity support in the event of financial market instability, which could lead to the expansion of the financial safety net. Besides, cross-border collateral would support more active cross-border banking since it would allow smoother financing by foreign banks and reduce settlement costs.

In addition, with global financial integration progressing, the use of LCY collateral could ease financial institutions' burden of holding assets and contribute to stabilizing the financial market by supplying settlement liquidity to financial institutions in a timely manner.

2. Contribution to the Secondary Market's Development

Activation of the use of collateral transactions by LCY bonds can not only improve the flow of funds but also contribute to the maturity and utilization of regional bond markets through the diversification of assets. If the functions of the collateral markets are facilitated, the financing channels of market participants could be diversified, which enables efficient allocation of capital in the market. In particular, if a collateral pool applied with the eligible criteria is established, a sound external trust base for government bonds could be strengthened. Cross-border collateral transactions also require the expansion of market infrastructures through linkages between real-time gross settlement (RTGS) and central securities depository (CSD) in the region, in which standardization such as ISO 20022 would pave the way.

All in all, the collateral transactions can mitigate credit risk and reduce financial costs, allowing a wider range of financial institutions to participate in the market. Accordingly, this would help stabilize the market by increasing market liquidity and creating more sound and active markets.

3. Expansion of Market Liquidity

Active use of LCY bonds held by investors in collateral transactions such as repo can increase the trading volume of bond transactions, leading to liquidity creation by market participants. In addition, if the central bank's eligible collateral is expanded to FCY-denominated bonds, market participants' financing resources could be expanded.

4. Reducing Financial Costs

If eligible collateral pools, including high-quality bonds, are expanded and cross-border financial transactions that utilize those pools grow, borrowers might have easier access to liquidity, which consequently may alleviate their financing costs. In addition, if the use of LCY bonds held in home economies is expanded through CBCA, financial institutions operating in host economies can secure channels that can directly raise liquidity there. Furthermore, market participants can reduce the cost of managing foreign exchange risk arising from currency mismatch with local currencies under the existing foreign exchange system built upon major currencies.

D. Impediments

In the survey, member institutions of CSIF indicated a number of constraints to cross-border collateral transactions. These include the lack of local bond market development, insufficient public disclosure of relevant laws and regulations, foreign-exchange-related restrictions and constraints, insufficient market infrastructures for cross-border transactions, and limited disclosure of relevant market information, among others. More efforts should be made to accurately identify various impediments and resolve them through close cooperation between authorities and market participants in the region.

1. Structural Factors Affecting the Regional Bond Market

ADB annually surveys participants in the bond market on structural factors affecting the market of each economy.[22] Comparing the survey results of 2010 and 2020 (Figure 14), the market conditions have significantly improved. The settlement and custody item was found to have improved the most, and the market accessibility and transparency were also found to have improved. However, the diversity of investors and hedging mechanisms have rather deteriorated.

According to the 2020 survey results (based on the average score of the nine economies surveyed), the score of the settlement and custody item was the highest at 3.69, followed by transparency at 3.43. The weakest score was for hedging mechanisms at 2.70, while market participation diversity stood just above this at 2.92 (Table 7).

Summing up the ADB bond market survey results, the development of hedging mechanisms for managing foreign exchange risk from nonresidents' investment and the diversity of local bond market participants were recognized as important tasks in the region.

---

[22]   This survey includes nine regional markets: the People's Republic of China; Hong Kong, China; Indonesia; the Republic of Korea; Malaysia; the Philippines; Singapore; Thailand; and Viet Nam.

Figure 14: Local Currency Bond Market Liquidity Survey in ASEAN+3
(Government Bond Market Structural Issues)

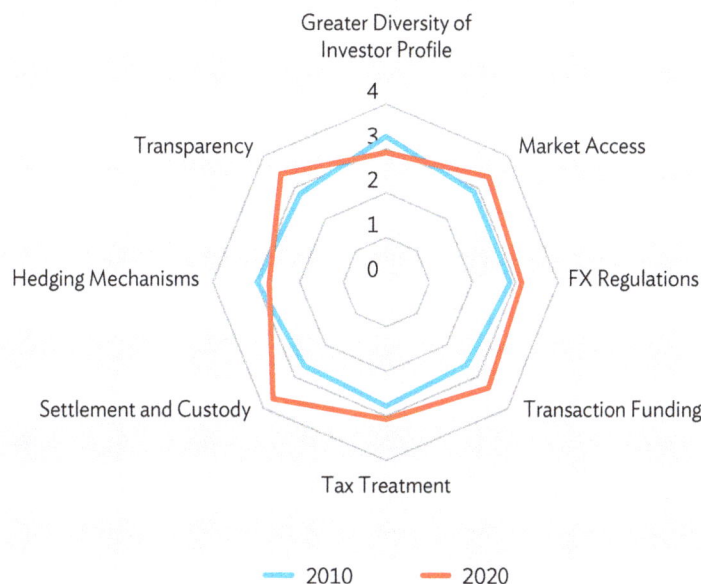

ASEAN+3 = Association of Southeast Asian Nations plus the People's Republic of China, Japan, and the Republic of Korea; FX = foreign exchange.
Source: ADB. AsianBondsOnline. Data Portal. https://asianbondsonline.adb.org/data-portal/.

Table 7: Evaluation of the State of Liquidity by Market Participants in Selected Markets, 2020
(Government Bond Market Structural Issues)

	CN	HK	ID	KR	MY	PH	SG	TH	VN	Average
Greater Diversity of Investor Profile	3.5	2.0	3.3	3.7	3.0	2.5	3.0	3.0	2.3	2.92
Market Access	3.0	4.0	3.5	3.7	3.3	2.8	3.5	3.3	3.0	3.34
FX Regulations	3.0	4.0	3.5	3.3	2.8	2.7	3.5	3.0	2.6	3.16
Transaction Funding	3.5	3.0	3.3	3.7	3.3	2.5	3.5	4.0	3.3	3.34
Tax Treatment	3.0	4.0	3.0	2.7	3.8	1.3	4.0	3.0	2.8	3.07
Settlement and Custody	3.5	4.0	3.3	4.0	4.0	3.5	4.0	4.0	2.9	3.69
Hedging Mechanisms	3.0	2.5	2.3	3.3	2.5	2.3	3.5	3.0	1.9	2.70
Transparency	3.0	2.5	3.3	4.0	4.0	3.3	4.0	3.7	3.1	3.43
Total	**25.5**	**26.0**	**25.5**	**28.4**	**26.7**	**20.9**	**29.0**	**27.0**	**21.9**	**25.66**

CN = People's Republic of China; FX = foreign exchange; HK = Hong Kong, China; ID = Indonesia; KR = Republic of Korea; MY = Malaysia; PH = Philippines; SG = Singapore; TH = Thailand; VN = Viet Nam.
Note: Scores range from 1 (poor) to 4 (excellent).
Source: ADB. AsianBondsOnline. Data Portal. https://asianbondsonline.adb.org/data-portal/.

2. Constraints to Cross-Border Collateral Transactions

The development of cross-border collateral markets has been affected by a number of factors. To identify the issues in the region, this study had conducted a survey targeting the CSIF member institutions. The survey responses from member institutions and additional information from the public and industry experts reflected that there are barriers in the region in the context of the circulation of high-quality bonds as collateral.

Each impediment that respondents identified as a constraint to increasing cross-border collateral transactions will be covered in detail below.

a. Lack of Local Bond Market Development

Generally, it was observed that the role of the bond market related to collateral financing remains low in the region. In particular, the development of the collateral market, which operates based on the evaluation of bonds value, is limited. The overall competence remains at a standstill due to weak motivation for market assessment of collateral itself. Though demand for bonds as collateral for direct financing instruments is rising, market conditions are still insufficient.

In the survey, respondents in several member economies assessed that their respective bond markets were well developed. However, some members responded that their bond markets and related market infrastructures, regulations, and practices were not sufficiently in place. In particular, respondents in these economies indicated a lack of market participant diversification as a challenging factor. Other member economies pointed out that there are difficulties in borrowing bonds for a sufficient period of time due to a lack of market liquidity available and restrictions on the reuse of collateral in repo transactions.

Another issue is related to the tax treatment. According to the survey, interest income and capital gains from bond investment are taxed in some economies. Imposing taxes on interest income from bond investment on nonresidents may adversely affect market liquidity by discouraging foreign participation in the secondary market, thereby increasing transaction costs and reducing active bond trading opportunities. Taking this into consideration, most emerging and advanced markets, by providing an exemption from taxes, are encouraging nonresidents to invest in their LCY-denominated bonds.

b. Insufficient Public Disclosure of Relevant Laws and Regulations

The transparent and robust legal framework of collateral transactions is the foundation on which the financial market involving collateral resides. In particular, repurchase agreements are generally characterized by having the full legal ownership title of collateral. In such a case with the event of a counterparty default, the full legal ownership title provides the buyer with the rights, thereby granting the right to reuse and protecting the investor's rights. However, this legal characteristic may not be clear in some markets. This would make it difficult for foreign investors to participate in the market especially if the legal framework for regulating the collateral differs across the region. The lack of certainty in contract fulfillment due to the use of non-standardized documents raises a concern that can hinder creditor protection in the event of default or bankruptcy. While improving the legal and regulatory frameworks in certain economies may be difficult, the disclosure of detailed laws and regulations for investor protection are important factors to build confidence in the collateral market.

In the survey, respondents in some member economies responded that there were no specific restrictions or regulations on collateral transactions, particularly cross-border collateral transactions. However, there seem to be significant differences in the level of disclosure of related laws and regulatory frameworks. It may be difficult and quite expensive to obtain legal certainty about how such laws actually work or how they will be interpreted by relevant legal jurisdictions.

Several member economies raised the absence of a single platform where legal and regulatory information could be easily obtained. They also pointed out that the transparency of regulations is very important for nonresidents who are unfamiliar with the domestic market and have language barriers. Searching costs for regulations that apply to nonresident investors should not be underestimated. The need has been raised for all member economies to disclose in detail the regulatory frameworks for bond transactions, preferably in an internationally common language, making it easier for foreign investors to understand.

c. Foreign-Exchange-Related Restrictions and Constraints

Among the factors that hinder nonresident participation in the local market, capital movement measures can be a critical issue because it impacts foreign investors' market access. Since the 1997/98 Asian financial crisis, regional economies have adopted various measures on capital transactions and have improved a lot, but still maintain some regulations. For example, regulations such as controls on cross-border transactions of local bonds and restrictions on foreign exchange positions of domestic financial institutions are in place to manage capital flow in both directions.

The survey found that some member economies have restrictions on cross-border transactions involving their LCY-denominated bonds. For example, local financial institutions are limited to offshore transactions of more than a certain amount. The survey results also indicate that some markets impose certain requirements on nonresidents purchasing local bonds. Nonresidents seeking LCY investments are required to undergo pre-reporting procedures to regulators in some regional markets. Some other markets impose a high level of restrictions on capital outflows, although nonresidents' capital inflows into their own markets are not constrained. These asymmetric regulations have caused a lack of motivation of participation by nonresidents, which is a limiting factor in access to LCY bond markets.

In the region, if there are no means of avoiding foreign exchange risk because of different currencies, foreign investors are forced to be exposed to foreign exchange rate risk as well as credit risk when trading LCY bonds. Therefore, the availability of hedging tools is particularly important to foreign investors.

Similarly, in the ADB annual survey of market participants, the lowest score in LCY bond markets was the lack of foreign exchange hedging mechanisms. These circumstances make it difficult for foreign investors to access regional LCY bond markets.[23]

---

[23] On the other hand, in the People's Republic of China, Bond Connect (Northbound) is operated to support foreign investors' transactions of LCY bonds. It supports cross-border trading between onshore market makers and offshore institutional investors. Bond Connect offers offshore investors access to all bonds in the China Inter-Bank Bond Market, namely, bonds with all types of credit ratings.

d. Insufficient Market Infrastructures for Cross-Border Transactions

The survey results show that most of the local clearing and settlement infrastructures for local bond transactions are well established. However, market infrastructures for activating the cross-border collateral market are still insufficient, and respondents in one economy responded that the current infrastructure was only designated to handle government bonds. Respondents in another economy mentioned the absence of local custodian banks as an obstacle.

Meanwhile, global market participants pointed out that market infrastructures are fragmented and not well connected in the region, resulting in high transaction costs, operational risks, and inefficient settlement in cross-border collateral transactions. Currently, regional CSDs are looking for mutual links, but in reality, most markets have cross-border financial transactions through global service providers.

Another constraint is that the settlement cycle varies from market to market. The bond settlement cycle in the regional market is mainly T+1 or T+2, but can range from T+0 to T+2. Global market experts pointed out that different settlement cycles between markets could hamper the activation of regional bond transactions for foreign investors (Table 8).

Table 8: Bond Market Settlement Cycle in ASEAN+3

Economy	Settlement Cycle
People's Republic of China	T+0 ~ T+1 (China Inter-Bank Bond Market Basis)
Hong Kong, China	T+2
Indonesia	T+2
Japan	Listed: T+2, OTC: T+1
Republic of Korea	T+1 (Negotiable)
Malaysia	T+2
Philippines	T+1
Singapore	T+2
Thailand	T+2 (Negotiable)
Viet Nam	T+1

ASEAN+3 = Association of Southeast Asian Nations plus the People's Republic of China, Japan, and the Republic of Korea; OTC = over-the-counter.
Sources: Cross-Border Settlement Infrastructure Forum Survey (2021); ADB. *ASEAN+3 Bond Market Guides*.

e. Limited Disclosure of Relevant Market Information

Market participants could find it difficult to access the necessary information—such as bonds prices, trading volume, credit ratings, financial reports, and investor protection rules—needed to conduct collateral transactions owing to a lack of transparency and disclosure. Investor protection and information disclosure are significant factors for foreign investors when they consider entering emerging markets. Nonresident market participants cannot determine who and where they can trade, so there can be practical barriers to cross-border collateral transactions. In addition, a lack of sufficient disclosure in the transactions may hinder the activation of the collateral market. Therefore, both the same level of investor protection and disclosure of relevant market information need to be applied to foreign investors as to domestic investors.

Foreign investors need to gather more information to understand and validate possible transactions. In addition, near-real-time reliability of price information on bonds pledged are also important issues for foreign investors. The price data should be readily available in most markets based on abundant transaction volume, and creditability should generally be established. A lack of market information sometimes makes it difficult to verify the accuracy of prices for certain types of bonds.

In the survey, some member economies pointed out that there was not enough disclosure of regulatory and market-related information. Some institutions presented the absence of a single platform that comprehensively provides information about the bond markets, and saw the level and content of information disclosure that differs from market to market as a constraint factor.

CSIF member institutions also raised the language barrier as another obstacle. Foreign investors find it difficult to verify accurate and timely regulatory information, and it is costly to implement document requirements. Therefore, access to information is a very important issue for nonresidents who are unfamiliar with the local markets and languages.

V

CONSIDERATIONS IN PROMOTING CROSS-BORDER COLLATERAL TRANSACTIONS

The use of LCY bonds for cross-border collateral transactions could help develop the region's bond markets by reducing the liquidity costs of financial institutions and expanding market liquidity. However, the overall benefits of the use of LCY bonds as collateral depend on a number of factors such as the regulatory frameworks, the environment of the domestic financial market, and cross-border market infrastructures.

Furthermore, in order to facilitate cross-border collateral transactions, a number of other factors need to be taken into account. These range from systemic risks that could cause a contagion of adverse impacts, legal and regulatory frameworks that could lead to varying levels of legal uncertainties, capacity of central bank business and market infrastructures, and market interconnectedness that could create interdependency.

In addition, there are conflicting issues between factors. For instance, introducing CBCAs can increase market efficiency by alleviating systemic risk and easing collateral constraints on financial institutions; but on the other hand, it can also add operational risks by expanding interconnectedness between financial market infrastructures and increasing interdependency among central banks.

A. Systemic Risk

Activating cross-border collateral transactions may increase market liquidity and lower financing costs, while the wider use of collateral composed of risk-free sovereign bonds in cross-border financial transactions could reduce the possibility of systemic risk. However, financial transactions are closely linked to each other. If collateral is reused, the linkage of financial transactions may further increase. The great integration of regional financial markets may lead to contagion risks where a problem in one economy could trigger chain reactions in other economies.

For instance, if the use of CBCAs expands, internationally active financial institutions may have more incentive to maintain as little collateral holdings in each operating market as possible. However, in the event of an unexpected simultaneous shock in a financial market, the risk of default on account of the lack of available collateral from financial institutions in particular markets would spread quickly to other markets. Therefore, robust risk management frameworks in relation to collateral valuation and margining would become more crucial.

B. Legal and Regulatory Frameworks

Solid and transparent regulatory frameworks related to cross-border collateral are an important foundation for the development of bond markets. However, cross-border collateral transactions may lead to varying levels of legal uncertainty. It is therefore essential for market participants to be fully aware of the legal risks posed by jurisdictions to regulate cross-border collateral transactions.

Another legal issue is settlement finality. It is a particularly relevant issue in cross-border transactions in which bonds move through different markets into book-entry systems. Clarity should be ensured when the settlement-related instruction of the collateral reaches its final destination. While most regional economies identify these issues and ensure a high level of certainty, such confidence may be more difficult to achieve in complex cross-border transactions.

C. Central Bank Capacities and Market Infrastructures

In promoting cross-border financial transactions that involve collateral, the policy capacities of central banks and the role of the market infrastructures are very important. For example, in the case of CBCA, as central banks become direct counterparties to the arrangement, the central banks providing liquidity undertake all risks in relation to the foreign collateral management. Consequently, the risks and burdens of the central banks could be very high.

Owing to the nature of CBCA in which foreign CSDs participate, there is also a high possibility of operational risk stemming from the complex linkages between market infrastructures. In addition, as at least two economies' pertinent laws and regulations apply to the use of foreign collateral, there could be legal friction between economies.

In order for cross-border collateral to move smoothly and for final settlements to be ensured, efficient and safe market infrastructures are essential. Only when the market infrastructures support these transactions might the transaction be vitalized.

As such, the capability of central banks and market infrastructures to take a leading role in such complex and highly interconnected collateral transactions is a critical consideration.

D. Market Interdependency

A potential problem of cross-border collateral transaction is that they may increase the interdependence among markets. And the interconnectedness among financial markets is likely to spread rather than contain the external shock depending on the financial environment. Indeed, collateral transactions can provide safe and efficient liquidity across the region and enhance the development of clearing and settlement systems. However, interconnectedness may result in interdependencies among financial markets.

Therefore, when connecting markets for cross-border transactions, the market infrastructures, risk management mechanism, and other variables of each market should be carefully considered.

VI

POLICY RECOMMENDATIONS

The use of LCY bonds as cross-border collateral requires well-developed domestic bond markets and well-organized laws and regulatory frameworks. Therefore, the possibility of collateral transactions varies greatly depending on the level of development of each factor in each market. With regard to the size of the bond market, which is the one of the most important factors in collateral capacity, regional economies have achieved notable growth in terms of the issuance of bonds. However, the secondary market, which allows bonds to be used as collateral, remains inadequate in most of the region. In emerging markets, repo transactions tend to be undertaken primarily with the central banks. After creating sufficient transactions with them, interbank collateral transactions might witness gradual increase.

This report proposes seven policy recommendations for promoting the cross-border use of LCY bonds as collateral in the ASEAN+3 region. Recommendations include developing LCY bond markets, enhancing disclosure of regulatory frameworks and market information, improving market infrastructures to address constraints identified through the survey, and taking into account considerations raised in Chapter V. In addition, a more active role from regional central banks is needed to enhance the use of LCY bonds. The linkages between market infrastructures could also be an ultimate way to promote collateral transactions. Finally, the activation of existing, but inactive, arrangements such as CBCA and QABs, would also enable the facilitation of cross-border financial transactions.

A. Recommendation 1: Further Development of the Local Currency Bond Markets

As analyzed in Chapter II, there are notable differences between member economies in terms of economic size and bond market development. In addition, the volume of bond issuance is large in much of the region, but trading volumes are not abundant and, accordingly, turnover ratios remain low. In particular, government bonds, a key asset of each economy, have been less prevalent in cross-border transactions due to careful capital inflow and outflow management related to growth strategies that value foreign exchange rate stability.

Fragmented market infrastructure in the region is another limitation. For instance, in some member economies, RTGSs and CSDs are in operation, but actual delivery-versus-payment (DVP) is not being implemented. Cross-border links between local market infrastructures that could efficiently support cross-border financial transactions are in operation but limited.

In the survey, respondents in several economies pointed out the insufficient development of their respective domestic bond markets as a constraint. Others also raised a few factors, including insufficient market efficiency and lack of transparency in laws and regulations, and others. It was also pointed out that complexity associated with tax credits and deductions and insufficient disclosure of detailed taxation arrangements could be barriers.

A well-functioning domestic bond market is one of the key stepping-stones for supporting efficient cross-border collateral transactions. In particular, the collateral market relies on liquidity provided by robust government bond markets. Looking at these factors comprehensively, boosting cross-border transactions requires that the domestic bond market be further developed as the first step.

Potential measures to support domestic bond market growth are as follows:

- Development of government bond markets, which are benchmarks in the LCY bond market, should be prioritized. It would build a foundation for the development of bond markets.

- A domestic interbank bond market can lead the development of the whole bond market. The interbank bond market in this respect is defined as a market in which financial institutions, banks in particular, generate cash or procure bonds on a short- or medium-term basis using collateral financing schemes, namely repos or reverse repos. It generally takes the form of an OTC market based on the necessity to cater to participants' diverse hedging or financing needs across different maturities. The interbank bond market can be a fundamental basis for reliable and timely availability of market interest rates (for discounting and valuation) provided that sufficient market liquidity is supported by participating financial institutions. However, in some economies, interbank bond transactions are not active. Given the critical functions of the interbank bond market, furthering its development across economies in the region would obviously be one of the priorities to facilitate regional cross-border collateral transactions.

- It is imperative to lay the foundation for a diverse range of investors to participate in an LCY bond market. It is also essential to remove redundant regulatory barriers to foreign investors' entry into the domestic market and enhance foreign exchange market access for foreign exchange risk hedging.

- The establishment of the HQLA-centered eligible pool that can be used as collateral is of critical significance.

- It is necessary to enable market participants to analyze and assess counterparty risks in the marketplace. In order to support this measure, relevant infrastructures that provide price information, bond transaction data, credit ratings, and financial reports of bond issuers need to be expanded.

- More efforts are needed to support the repo trading market for collateral transactions. Looking at the regional collateral market structure, repo transactions account for more than 97% of total collateral transactions. As such, repo transactions are central to the collateral market. The vitalization of repo transactions would assist the domestic bond market development by enhancing secondary market liquidity and expanding investor participation. These tasks include improving the protection of creditors' rights in legal frameworks, adopting standardized documents such as the Global Master Repurchase Agreement.

- Taxing jurisdictions may differ on the rates of income or gain taxes from bond transactions, scope of taxable income, and the rules on situs of taxation, among others. These differences may be reconciled through treaty agreements between economies.

- Currently, diverse measures for regional bond market development are being discussed in the four task forces under the Asian Bond Markets Initiatives. However, more specific discussions of how LCY bonds could be considered as collateral in cross-border transactions and how liquidity and eligibility could be expanded are needed as well.

B. Recommendation 2: Disclosure Enhancement of Regulatory Frameworks and Market Information

According to the Principle 23 (disclosure of rules, key procedures, and market data) of the Principles for Financial Market Infrastructures (PFMI) established by the BIS Committee on Payment and Market Infrastructures and the International Organization of Securities Commissions (IOSCO), financial market infrastructure (FMI) should provide sufficient information to enable participants to have an accurate understanding of the risks, fees, and other material costs they incur by participating in the FMI. All relevant rules and key procedures should be publicly disclosed.[24]

In the survey, the constraints most frequently raised by international market experts and member institutions were the limited disclosure of market information and regulatory frameworks.

Meanwhile, in the annual survey conducted by ADB, transparency improved significantly in 2020 compared to 2010, recording the second-highest score among all market infrastructure factors. From these results, transparency can be seen as being much improved.

ADB also provides *ASEAN+3 Bond Market Guides* that contain detailed information on the bond market of each economy through the bond market portal, *AsianBondsOnline,* which is aimed at helping nonresident investors collect data and reference materials for their investments. Each economy's bond market guide includes information concerning the legal and regulatory framework, key characteristics and developments of the LCY bond markets, and pertinent market infrastructures. Furthermore, *AsianBondsOnline* serves as a one-click source of various information on bond markets in the ASEAN+3 region. In view of this, *AsianBondsOnline* and the bond market guides are good platforms for foreign investors to collect investment information of the region.

Nevertheless, market participants are still calling for transparency in the regulatory framework and further disclosure of market information for each member in its economy. Disclosure of general market information including transaction and settlement status of bond transactions would be another critical enabler for the active use of cross-border collateral upon LCY bonds. In this regard, it would be desirable for each economy to disclose pertinent information in a more comprehensive and transparent manner, such as laws, regulatory frameworks, and market information.

Specific measures to implement these tasks are as follows:

- As indicated by the PFMI, FMIs should publicly disclose sufficient market information along with relevant rules and key procedures. Therefore, it would be desirable to build a single platform in each economy where all information—including price information, bond transaction data, credit ratings, financial reports of bond issuers, and taxation arrangements—can be collected in one place.

- Information needs to be released in as much detail as possible using the international common language to help foreign investors understand it easily.

- It is also important to establish a framework that can monitor market information such as changes in various regulations and bonds prices by expanding information exchange between economies.

---

[24]   BIS CPMI-IOSCO. 2012. *Principles for Financial Market Infrastructures.* Basel, pp. 121–123.

C. Recommendation 3: Enhancement of Cross-Border Market Infrastructures

In the survey, several member economies and market experts pointed out that the market infrastructures for domestic bond transactions are well in place, but the infrastructures for cross-border collateral transactions are far from sufficient. Cross-border financial transactions are greatly influenced by efficiency of domestic market infrastructures. Clearing and settlement systems for cross-border collateral transactions are essential components of developing broad and liquid regional collateral markets.

Cross-border collateral market functions are dependent upon an efficient and flexible collateral management scheme supported by stable operations of financial market infrastructures. Therefore, it is imperative to enhance domestic market infrastructures through the following measures:

- The enhancement of market infrastructure functions including collateral management services and DVP needs to be accelerated. Well-functioning CSDs and SSSs can contribute to the wider availability of cross-border transactions by enabling efficient collateral management services. For example, CCDC in the People's Republic of China provides collateral management services such as cross-border financing, cross currency swap, and FCY interbank securities financing to promote the use of LCY bonds (Figure 15). Well-established CSDs and SSSs also contribute to secure collateral transactions through more robust valuation and estimation frameworks, which are essential for risk management. This implies that the active mobilization of the LCY bonds across the region relies heavily on the reliability of market infrastructures.

- In terms of improving the efficiency of collateral transactions and mitigating risks, actual cross-border DVP schemes need to be further supported by viable linkage networks of CSDs and RTGSs.

Figure 15: **Collateral Management Service Structure of Central Securities Depository**

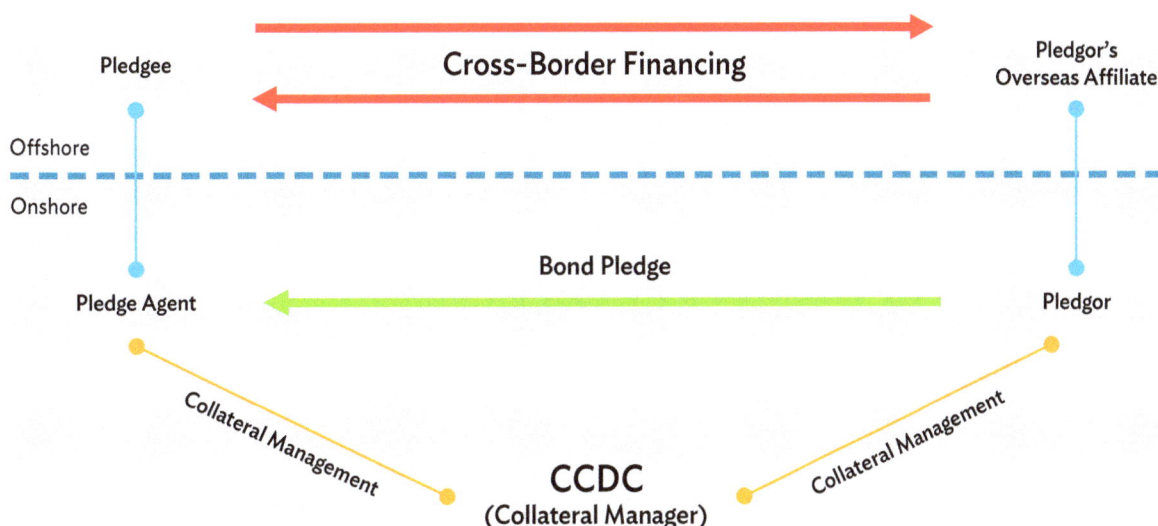

CCDC = China Central Depository & Clearing Co., Ltd.
Source: CCDC. 2021. *Collateral Management Service.* Beijing.

- Introducing international technical standards and harmonizing the settlement cycle between economies are also needed. In particular, shortening the settlement cycle is an important issue in securing the stability of transactions in cross-border collateral. This is because the longer the settlement period after a bond trade, the more risk exposure that market participants have to bear. In order to shorten the settlement cycle, infrastructure enhancement efforts such as reforming market practices, automating work, and introducing international standards need to be taken into account.

- In addition, shortening a settlement cycle for intraregional transaction may increase a possibility for LCY bonds to be utilized as collateral. Normally, cross-border transactions are settled in T+2 because of the time difference among different regions such as the US. Since ASEAN+3 economies are in similar time zones, market infrastructure linkages can enable same-day transactions, which would be critical for liquidity management.

D. Recommendation 4: Wider Linkages between Regional Market Infrastructures

CSIF member institutions and market experts pointed out that cross-border financial transactions are still inefficient partly due to the lack of linkages between market infrastructures. In the case of the euro area, active collateral mobilization across the countries is available because of close linkages between market infrastructures as well as the use of a single currency. Therefore, in order to promote use of LCY bonds for cross-border collateral and operational risk reduction, more linkages among market infrastructures to enable straight-through-processing (STP) might be needed.

1. Strengthening the Linkages between Market Infrastructures

Linkages between financial market infrastructures among member economies need to be enhanced to facilitate cross-border collateral transactions. The expansion of linkages could ease the mobilization of LCY bonds and reduce operational risk. Currently, market infrastructures in this region are not well linked, which may lead to delaying settlement timing and increasing transaction costs. Enhancing interconnectivity among financial market infrastructures can improve efficiency, strengthen risk management, and reduce financing costs.

As described in detail in Chapter II, the CSD–RTGS linkage between market infrastructures is a representative example. It can not only reduce transaction costs, but also mitigate concerns of collateral shortage by enabling DVP and mobilizing LCY bonds as collateral. Since the ASEAN+3 bond market operates in the same (or adjacent) time zone, regional CSD–RTGS linkages can generate additional market liquidity.

Meanwhile, in the euro area, the Target 2 and the Target 2 Securities that support smooth cross-border financial transactions are well established. However, in the region, there are currently only links between CSD–RTGS or CSD–CSD. In order to expand the linkages, CSD and RTGS in one economy and those in another economy need to be connected simultaneously to achieve substantial DVP. This issue also needs to be discussed at the CSIF meetings in the future.

2. Adoption of International Standards

It is important to broadly adopt international standards such as ISO 20022 to increase settlement efficiency and reduce the operational risks in cross-border transactions. Some member economies are in the process of or are planning to fully adopt ISO 20022 to support the interoperability of market infrastructures.

3. Straight-Through-Processing

Interoperability between regional financial market infrastructures is also important for realizing STP in cross-border financial transactions. STP could help improve settlement processing and efficiency, and reduce operational risk.

E. Recommendation 5: Expansion of Central Banks' Role in Cross-Border Collateral Management

The impact of the central bank collateral frameworks on cross-border transactions—including collateral availability, bond prices, and market practices—is of critical significance. In particular, central bank policy measures assessing and deciding on asset eligibility, haircut ratio, and accessibility to counterparties could have a decisive impact on cross-border collateral management practices.

The BIS has indicated the "eligibility policies," "range of counterparties," and "rationale/range of operations" as aspects of a central bank's policy for collateral markets. It also pointed out "collateral acceptance" and "managing policy" as the focal point of a central bank's eligibility policy for collateral markets (Figure 16).

Figure 16: Effects of Central Bank Policy on Collateral Markets
(% of total respondents)

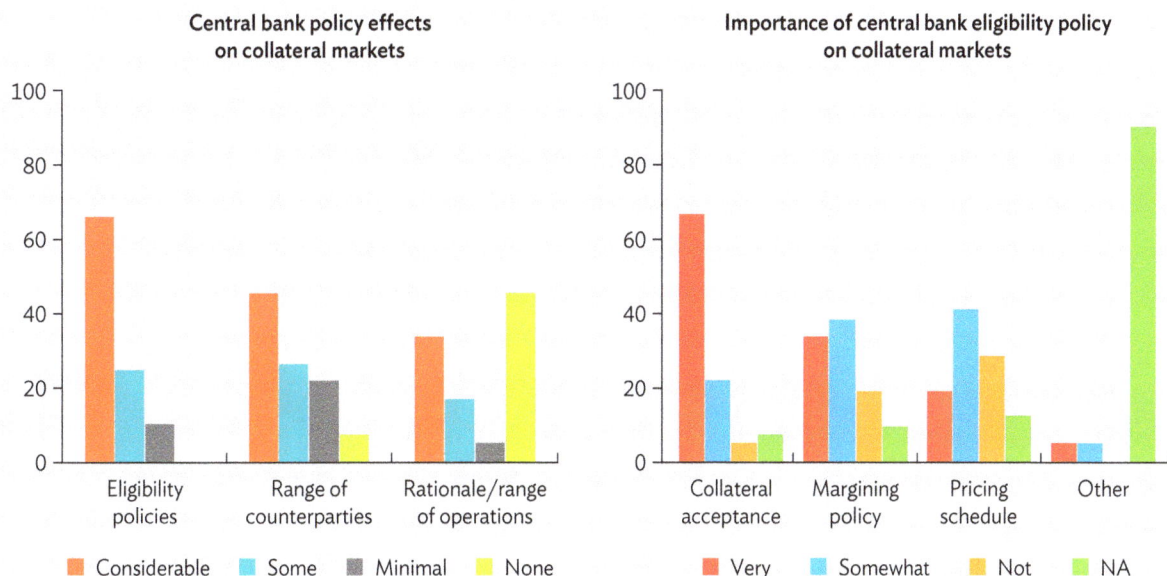

NA = not applicable.

Source: Bank for International Settlements. 2015. *Central Bank Operating Frameworks and Collateral Markets*. Basel.

Specific measures to expand the role of central banks in promoting cross-border collateral transactions are as follows:

- The role of central banks in building the collateral framework is traditionally significant. Furthermore, the expansion of eligibility is an important factor in enhancing the collateral capabilities. Consequently, central banks, which have a decisive impact on the supply and use of collateral, need to lead the establishment of collateral eligibility, expansion of qualifying collateral pools, and upgrading of asset price assessment systems.

- With the exception of some member economies that accept FCY-denominated bonds as collateral for liquidity support in operating economies, most central banks' lists are limited to domestic bonds. If regional central banks agreed to expand eligibility to include government and other eligible bonds of ASEAN+3 member economies, it could increase cross-border bond transactions, improving market liquidity and strengthening financial stability.[25]

F. Recommendation 6: Expansion of Cross-Border Collateral Arrangements

The BIS suggested the active domestic bond markets, close links between financial markets, and the participation of internationally active financial institutions in the market infrastructures as key factors for success of CBCA.[26]

Since the euro area uses a single currency, national central banks can not only easily reflect the value of collateral in its accounting books but also eliminate the foreign exchange risk when accepting foreign collateral. This contributes to the active utilization of CBCA in the euro area. In addition, the ease of cross-border mobilization of collateral with the establishment of the Target 2 payment system and the Target 2 Securities settlement system play an important role in the spread of CBCA. Therefore, even if the eligible collateral is located outside the economy, these well-established market infrastructures enable the facilitation of the liquidity supply by accepting and verifying foreign collateral with ease.

As the benefits and issues of CBCA were analyzed in detail in Chapter III, CBCA can have diverse impacts such as increasing liquidity in the financial markets, developing the LCY bond markets, and expanding the financial safety net. Notwithstanding the desirable effects, however, there are some issues to be taken into account.

Therefore, it is of significance to consider expanding and facilitating the CBCA, and the following measures might be stepping-stones in addressing the issues and furthering CBCAs in the region:

- As Table 3 indicates, many regional central banks still do not recognize FCY-denominated bonds as eligible collateral. The central bank-led CBCA might be a valid policy tool for activating the cross-border collateral transactions. Therefore, the expansion of the central bank's eligible collateral criteria is crucial, in particular the expansion of asset pool to include FCY bonds.

---

[25] ADB. 2020. *Next Steps for ASEAN+3 Central Securities Depository and Real-Time Gross Settlement Linkages: A Progress Report of the Cross-Border Settlement Infrastructure Forum*, p. 31.

[26] BIS. 2006. *Cross-border collateral arrangements*. Basel.

- As discussed in detail in Chapter III, regional CBCAs remain in the readiness stage due to their inherent nature of emergency measures aimed at responding to financial turmoil. Therefore, continuously activating the operations of the current CBCAs are needed so that financial institutions could easily raise local liquidity on a routine basis.

- Well-functioning market infrastructures could enable the facilitation of CBCA. Therefore, it would be desirable to promote both the expansion of market infrastructures for custody, evaluation, and clearing and settlement of collateral bonds and more cross-border linkages among them in the region.

- In order to facilitate the CBCA by local financial institutions, the margin rate applied to CBCA should be aligned with ordinary policy rates. In addition, the rate should not be seen as a penalty.

- Central banks need to cooperate with other central banks that accept FCY bonds as collateral in providing liquidity to foreign financial institutions in its jurisdiction to strengthen monitoring such as valuation of collateral and to exchange information on financial market conditions.

- Under the principle of reciprocity when introducing CBCAs between advanced and emerging economies, it is necessary to promote bilateral contracts. This is to ensure that the bonds in emerging markets are recognized as eligible collateral in advanced countries, thereby making sure that financial institutions in emerging markets could benefit from the system.

- Since there are various models for CBCA implementation as illustrated in Appendix 1, it is necessary to select a model suitable for each economy's situation. For instance, if the market infrastructures are insufficient, introducing the tri-party CCBM that provides collateral management services across the markets may also be an alternative.

G. Recommendation 7: Facilitation of Qualified ASEAN Banks

One key agenda item of the ASEAN Economic Community is the integration of ASEAN financial markets.[27] QABs under the ASEAN Banking Integration Framework (ABIF) are intended to increase the openness of domestic financial markets to banks from other ASEAN member economies.

The ABIF allows domestic banks that meet certain criteria to gain more access to other ASEAN markets. Given the nature of QABs, it may have a positive effect on the increase of cross-border collateral transactions, while the reverse might also be true in that those transactions might be a catalyst for more active use of QABs in the region.

---

[27] As a part of efforts to enhance financial and economic integration in the ASEAN region, the Local Currency Settlement Framework (LCSF) was also launched. The LCSF is the settlement of bilateral transactions carried out by two economies using the local currency that prevails in each economy. This framework mainly aims to reduce dependence on the US dollar for bilateral trade transaction settlement and maintain the stability of domestic currencies in the ASEAN region. Key objectives of the LCSF include (i) enhancing regional financial integration among ASEAN countries, (ii) encouraging the use of local currency for trade settlement and direct investment, and (iii) mitigating currency risks arising from volatility of major currencies. Therefore, ASEAN member economies have initiated the LCSF as the FCY exchange system. Accordingly, this framework was outside the subject of this study.

According to the survey, there are three cases of bilateral QAB agreements between ASEAN economies:

1. QAB agreement between Otoritas Jasa Keuangan (OJK) Indonesia and the Bank Negara Malaysia (BNM),
2. QAB agreement between the BNM and the Bangko Sentral ng Pilipinas (BSP), and
3. QAB agreement between the BNM and the Bank of Thailand (BOT).

Currently, two QABs are in operation under the agreement between regional economies. However, in other agreements, QABs have not yet been executed so far. Overall, it seems that they are not yet widely implemented in the ASEAN region.

If, in particular, QABs are put in place in conjunction with CBCA, cross-border collateral transactions of LCY bonds might be further accelerated. Therefore, greater market access and operational flexibility for QABs through the ABIF needs to be considered.

VII

NEXT STEPS

In parallel with policy recommendations, this study proposes follow-up actions to be taken in the future in the context of further development of the regional cross-border collateral market. The next steps include (i) additional in-depth studies on the subject of the cross-border collateral financing, repo and other derivatives transactions, and comparative analysis of central banks' repo operations; (ii) support for market participants' activities; (iii) establishment of ASEAN+3 regional market and legal practices; (iv) close cooperation between authorities and related agencies for the expansion of regional cross-border financing and financial stability; and (v) establishment of working groups for constructing a road map.

A. In-Depth Study of Cross-Border Collateral Financing

There have not been many studies in the region on cross-border collateral financing. Through conducting the survey, the current status of bond markets and market infrastructures, and constraints related to cross-border collateral transactions were identified. Based on the analysis, policy recommendations were presented.

However, there was a limit to gathering sufficient information from all member markets. Information related to domestic collateral transactions is limited or often not available, while no information related to cross-border collateral transactions is available. This is because there is no system to collect the information; repo transactions are comingled with outright purchase transactions, and there may be no centralized collateral management system to gather the information.

To identify the current status of the collateral market, further in-depth study should be considered. Given the lack of comprehensive data compilation system regionally, the study requires careful designing. For example, it would be necessary to focus on some key areas such as the need for cross-border collateral financing, securities lending, and repo transactions in limited markets where cross-border transactions are active. In addition, comparative data collection and analysis on central banks' repo operations can be considered as a starting point of a regional discussion. These activities can address the notable differences, particularly on the size and relative growth of each bond market in the region.

B. Support for Market Participants' Collateral Activities

It is difficult for domestic financial institutions to actively enter cross-border financial transactions in regional markets. It is also difficult for emerging economies' financial institutions to use CBCA as a tool of financing LCY liquidity if bonds issued in emerging markets are not recognized as eligible collateral in developed markets. In addition, from the emerging market perspective, it is concerning that the expansion of the country's eligible collateral criteria to FCY-denominated bonds may reduce the competitiveness of domestic financial institutions with relatively weak collateral and operating networks as global financial institutions with wide networks strengthen their market activities.

However, various empirical studies suggest the entry of foreign banks and an increase in competition in the domestic banking market would promote innovation and enhance access to finance if properly regulated. Foreign banks tend to focus more on wholesale markets where big companies are active, while domestic banks continue to be dominant in retail markets where information asymmetry is high. Besides, foreign banks' operations are often focused on their national clients; thus, the impact on domestic banks' competitiveness may not be as high as expected. On the contrary, CBCA may reduce a burden of the host central bank when foreign banks face liquidity shortage because the central bank does not need to act as the lender of last resort to them.

Regional member economies have traditionally been passive in establishing collateral criteria focusing on safe assets and activating cross-border transactions with a top priority on financial market stability. As a result, efforts to incorporate eligible collateral in the global market were insufficient even though it was a government bond with high credit ratings.

These factors act as constraints on mobilizing collateral across markets and make it difficult for financial institutions to fund liquidity by pledging LCY bonds in the global market.

Accordingly, it is necessary to establish the open eligible collateral criteria for supporting business activities in the private sector, expand CBCAs based on reciprocity, and make efforts to incorporate government bonds into global eligible collateral.

C. Establishment of the ASEAN+3 Regional Market and Legal Practices

Regional markets tend to follow practices of developed markets because investors from developed markets are important to the region. However, the volume of bond issuances and transactions in the ASEAN+3 region are significantly increasing. Therefore, it is necessary to develop the market practices suitable for the Asian market environment. Furthermore, as mentioned above, since regional market practices are also important to foreign investors, harmony with global market practices is essential.

In addition, to reduce legal difference among member economies, Asian legal practices have to be established. Europe overcame this problem by issuing common legislation: the European Directives and Regulations. However, it is not easy to issue the same laws and regulations that could apply regionally. For this reason, it is imperative to establish ASEAN+3's own common legal practices to reduce legal uncertainty and complexity.

D. Close Cooperation between Authorities and Related Agencies for the Expansion of Regional Cross-Border Financing and Financial Stability

Under the environment where financial markets are connected and integrated, financial stability in one economy is directly linked to the stability in neighboring economies.

Furthermore, Responsibility E (Cooperation with other authorities) of the Principles for Financial Market Infrastructures (PFMI) established by BIS CPMI and IOSCO recommends that central banks, market regulators, and other relevant authorities should cooperate with each other, both domestically and internationally, as appropriate, in promoting the safety and efficiency of FMIs.[28]

Therefore, close cooperation between authorities and related agencies is more relevant to the expansion of regional cross-border financing and financial stability.

Specific measures for consideration are as follows:

- Close and supportive cooperation between policy authorities is needed to improve the interoperability of market infrastructures to contribute to risk mitigation and the further use of collateral.

- For central banks that introduce CBCA, it is important to have close cooperation and information-sharing between the region's central banks.

- It is essential to raise awareness of the importance of the cross-border collateral financing for the development of the domestic bond market as well as the sufficient disclosure of market information along with relevant rules and procedures. Therefore, immediate actions to be taken in this regard would be to further training programs, seminars, and meetings.

- Additional CSD–RTGS linkages, not just a link between CSDs but also with RTGS to ensure DVP, are needed. To this end, it is necessary to continuously discuss this agenda at the CSIF.

- CSIF needs to conduct a further study on the regulatory frameworks and market practices of developed economies and share with member institutions and market participants.

- Since the Asian Prime Collateral Forum is also studying topics related to collateral transactions, close cooperation between CSIF and the Asian Prime Collateral Forum seems required as well. For instance, the two forums could organize joint seminars on cross-border collateral markets.

---

[28]   BIS CPMI–IOSCO. 2012. *Principles for Financial Market Infrastructures.* Basel, pp. 133–137.

E. Establishment of Working Groups for Constructing a Road Map

As the survey results show, the constraints to the development of cross-border collateral markets are very complex. It is difficult to improve much in a short period of time because each member economy has a very different market environment and system. Besides, the level of capital market development also varies across regional economies. In addition, the unexpected issues such as the coronavirus disease (COVID-19) pandemic may adversely affect efforts toward the active use of LCY collateral for cross-border financial transactions in the region.

Taking these factors into account, it is essential to consider a mid- to long-term strategy and road map for the collateral market's development including the establishment of a timeline.

To this end, it is desirable to form a dedicated group of experts supported by CSIF member economies to undertake in-depth analysis of regional collateral issues. Given the degree of bond market development and market sizes of ASEAN+3 member economies, the study group should take a stepwise approach to involve all member economies. It is also necessary to refer to the case of global organizations, such as the BIS Committee on Payment and Market Infrastructures, forming small working groups for various agenda items and in-depth discussions among experts.

CROSS-BORDER COLLATERAL ARRANGEMENT MODELS

A. Correspondent Central Banking Model

The correspondent central banking model (CCBM) is a method in which the central bank of a country where collateral is located acts as a custodian bank if the whereabouts of bonds used as collateral and the whereabouts of liquidity actually supplied are different. This method can be divided into four types—standard CCBM, CCBM with links, tri-party CCBM, and guarantee CCBM—depending on the type of collateral management services.[1]

1. Standard Correspondent Central Banking Model

Under the standard CCBM, the central bank that acts as a custodian (the correspondent central bank, CCB) for the central bank that extends credit to its domestic counterparties (home central bank, HCB) accepts the collateral located in its local securities settlement system (SSS) on behalf of the HCB. Central banks may choose this model because it is a relatively simple model that relies on the existing account relationships between central banks.[2]

If a counterparty holds foreign currency (FCY) eligible assets in the foreign SSS in which these assets have been issued and wishes to use them as collateral with its HCB, it instructs the HCB and the SSS to transfer the assets to the central bank of the relevant foreign country (CCB) for the account of the HCB. The CCB provides the necessary information to the HCB on the delivery of the securities, while the HCB processes that information, conducts the valuation process (including margin calls and valuation haircuts), and provides liquidity to the counterparty. The HCB will not advance funds until it is certain that the mobilized securities have been safely received by the CCB on its behalf (Figure A1.1).

---

[1] The Bank for International Settlements (BIS) and the European Central Bank (ECB) published several reports explaining the cross-border collateral arrangement (CBCA) models. All descriptions related to the CBCA models in this appendix were cited from those reports.

[2] ECB. 2022. *Correspondent central banking model (CCBM) Procedures for Eurosystem counterparties.* Frankfurt, pp. 5–6; BIS. 2006. *Cross-border collateral arrangements.* Basel, pp. 21–22.

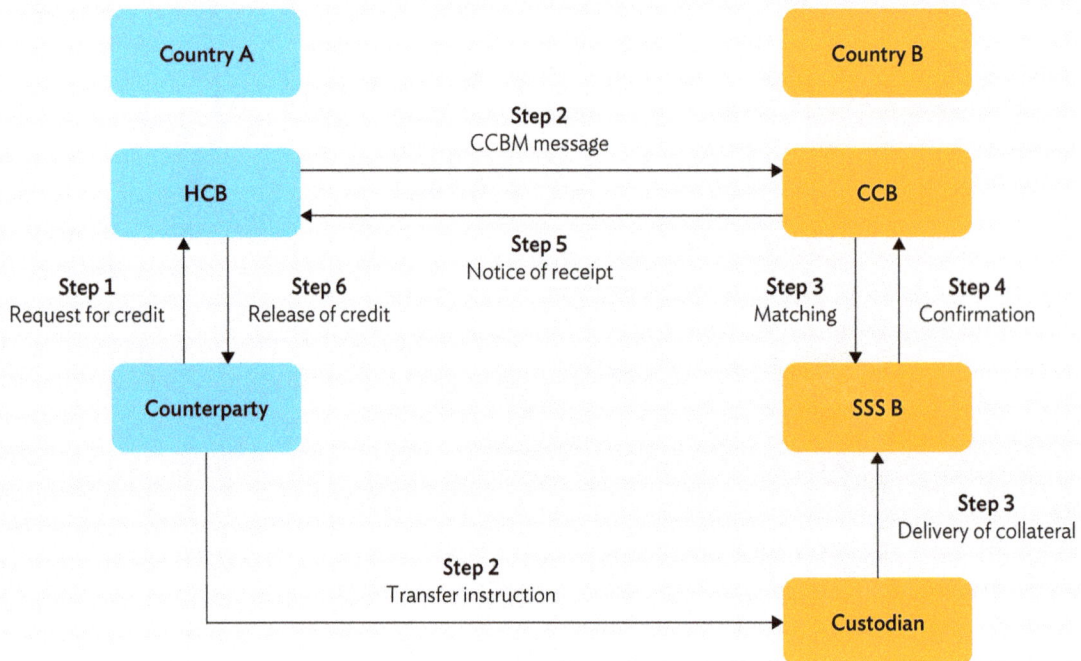

Figure A1.1: Standard Correspondent Central Banking Model

CCB = correspondent central bank, CCBM = correspondent central banking model, HCB = home central bank, SSS B = securities settlement system in Country B.
Source: European Central Bank. 2019. *Correspondent Central Banking Model Procedures for Eurosystem Counterparties.* Frankfurt.

2. Correspondent Central Banking Model with Links

This model has the same basic structure as standard CCBM, and is mainly utilized when the issuing and holding institutions of the collateral are different. The two countries' SSS can be very useful when they are interconnected.[3]

Under this arrangement, the HCB and its counterparts use an SSS "linked" to one or more SSSs. A link between two SSSs allows a participant in one SSS to hold securities issued in another SSS without being a participant in the latter. With links, the cross-border relationship is between the SSSs: they open omnibus accounts with one another.

Counterparties can use this model to mobilize eligible marketable assets held in an SSS other than the SSS in which the assets were issued, provided that an eligible link exists between the SSSs concerned.

If a counterparty wishes to collateralize eligible marketable assets with its HCB by making use of the CCBM with eligible link option, it instructs the HCB and the SSS in the country in which the assets are held to transfer the assets to the central bank of that country (CCB) for the account of the HCB (Figure A1.2).

---

[3]   ECB. 2022. *Correspondent central banking model (CCBM) Procedures for Eurosystem counterparties.* Frankfurt, pp. 7–8.

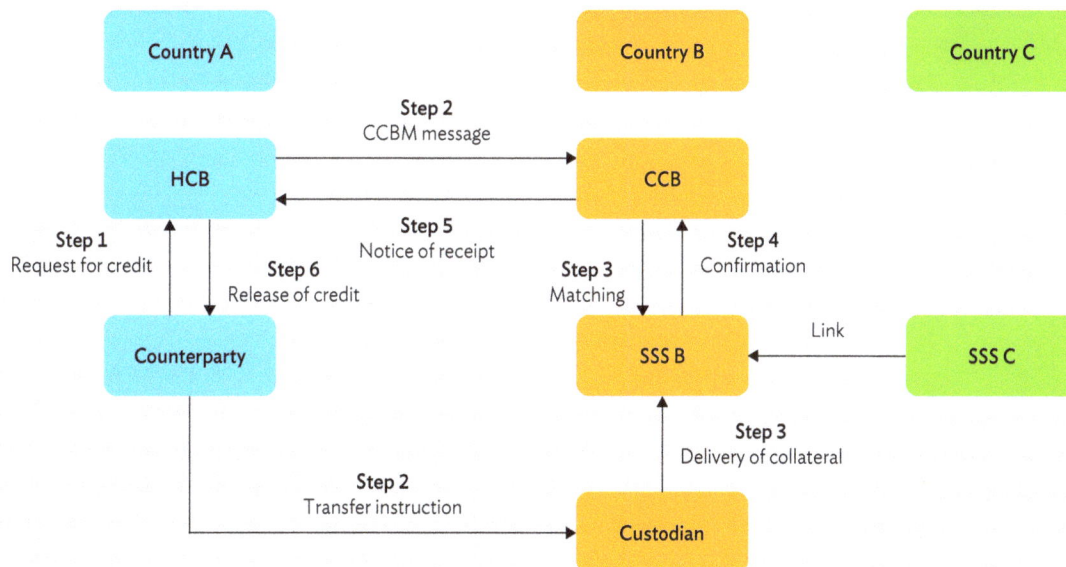

Figure A1.2: Correspondent Central Banking Model with Links

CCB = correspondent central bank, CCBM = correspondent central banking model, HCB = home central bank, SSS B = securities settlement system in Country B, SSS C = securities settlement system in Country C.

Source: European Central Bank. 2019. *Correspondent Central Banking Model Procedures for Eurosystem Counterparties.* Frankfurt.

3. Tri-Party Correspondent Central Banking Model

Under this arrangement, the HCB and its counterparties rely on a collateral management service (CMS). The CMS can take the form of a tripartite collateral service operated by an SSS or a custodian. Depending on the operator, the CMS could offer services for collateral issued in one or more countries. Therefore, the HCB must be able to rely on the quality and resilience of the infrastructure and processes of the CMS operator.[4]

This model provides a basis for the cross-border use of tri-party CMSs, whereby the CCB of a market where tri-party CMSs are being offered for cross-border use acts as a custodian for HCB with local counterparties wishing to take advantage of such services on a cross-border basis (Figure A1.3).

4. Guarantee Correspondent Central Banking Model

Under this arrangement, the CCB acts as a guarantor for the HCB with respect to assets pledged in its local depository or SSS.[5]

Importantly, the instrument backing this arrangement is a guarantee from the CCB on the value of collateral received. This instrument does not require the actual cross-border transfer of title to the collateral assets but rather the issuance of a cross-border inter-central bank guarantee (Figure A1.4).

---

[4]   ECB. 2022. *Correspondent central banking model (CCBM) Procedures for Eurosystem counterparties.* Frankfurt, pp. 8–9.

[5]   BIS. 2006. *Cross-border collateral arrangements.* Basel, p. 23.

Figure A1.3: Tri-Party Correspondent Central Banking Model

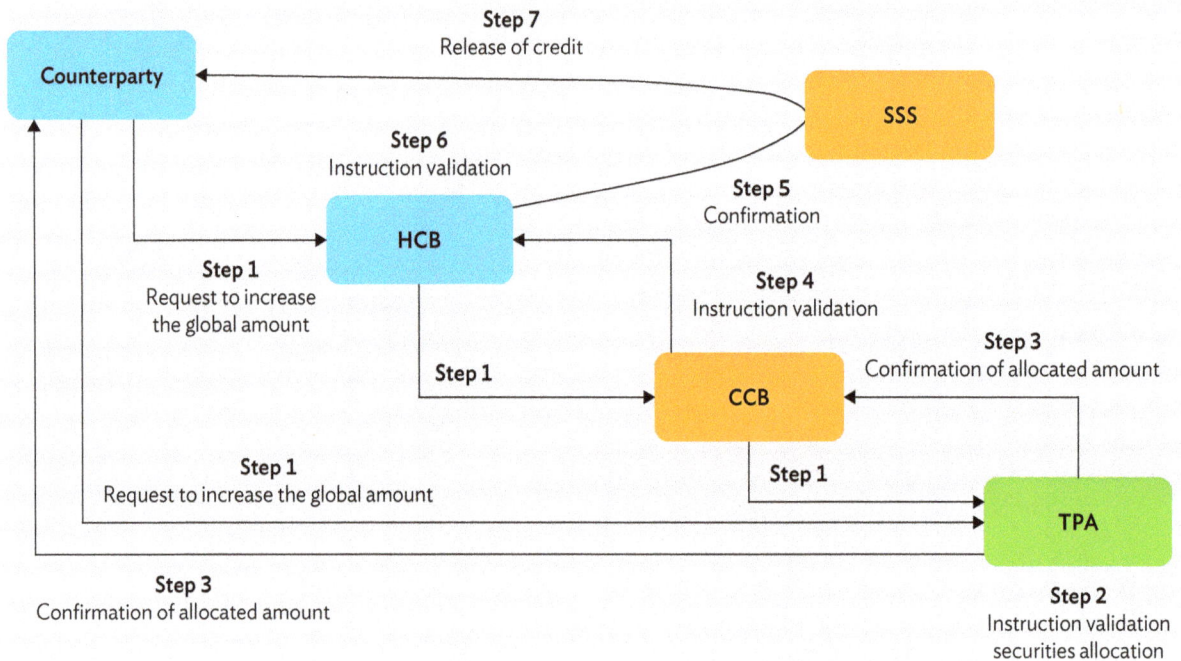

CCB = correspondent central bank, HCB = home central bank, SSS = securities settlement system, TPA = tri-party agency.
Source: European Central Bank. 2019. *Correspondent Central Banking Model Procedures for Eurosystem Counterparties.* Frankfurt.

Figure A1.4: Guarantee Correspondent Central Banking Model

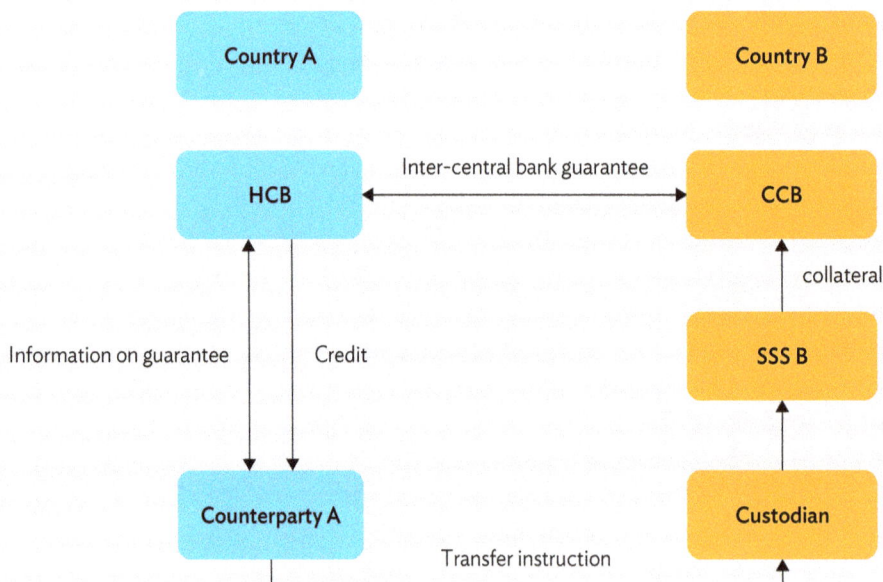

CCB = correspondent central bank, HCB = home central bank, SSS B = securities settlement system in Country B.
Source: Bank for International Settlements. 2006. *Cross-border collateral arrangements.* Basel.

B. Non-Correspondent Central Banking Model

Non-CCBMs can be utilized when the central bank of the lender (HCB) receives collateral directly using its market infrastructure such as CSD and supplies liquidity based on it, regardless of the central bank of the collateral-based country.

1. Direct Links

The model is used in which CSDs in both countries directly link the SSS without intermediaries to transfer collateral from the issuing institution to the investment institution (counterparty) and receive it as collateral by the HCB.[6]

This model is an account opened by an (I)CSD, referred to as the "investor SSS," in the books of another (I)CSD, referred to as the "issuer SSS," in order to facilitate the transfer of securities from participants in the issuer SSS to participants in the investor SSS.

The Direct Links implies that no intermediary exists between the two SSSs, and the operation of the omnibus account opened by the investor SSS is managed either by the investor SSS or the issuer SSS (Figure A1.5).[7]

Figure A1.5: Direct Links

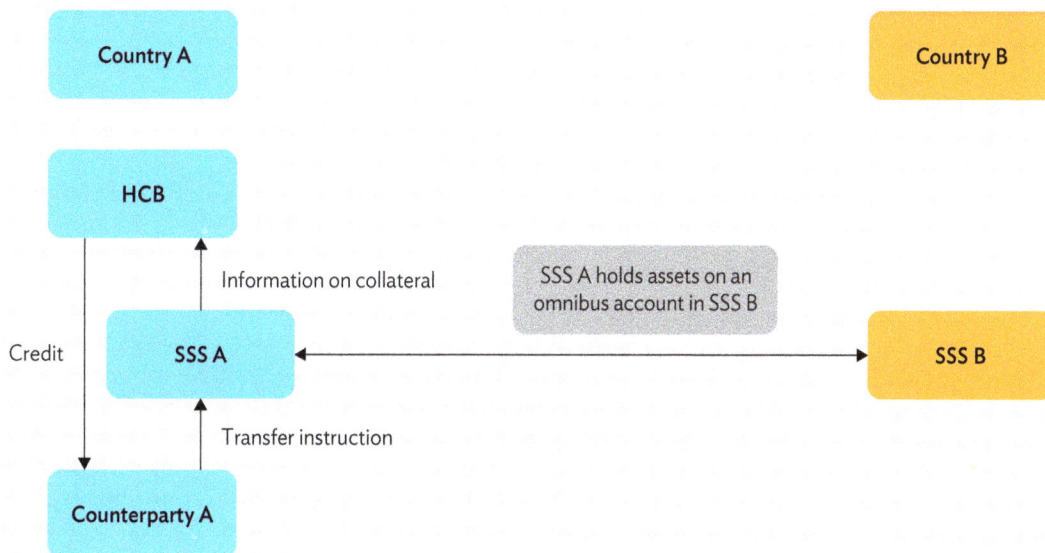

HCB = home central bank, SSS A = securities settlement system in Country A, SSS B = securities settlement system in Country B.
Source: European Central Bank. List of Eligible Links. Frankfurt. https://www.ecb.europa.eu/paym/coll/coll/ssslinks/.

---

[6] ECB. List of Eligible Links. Frankfurt. https://www.ecb.europa.eu/paym/coll/coll/ssslinks/; BIS. 2006. *Cross-border collateral arrangements*. Basel, pp. 23–24.

[7] A securities account opened by the "investor SSS" to "issuer SSS" for securities settlements by investors using internationsl SSSs through ICSD.

2. Relayed Links

Relayed Links is a contractual and technical arrangement for the transfer of securities involving at least three SSSs: the "investor" SSS, the "issuer" SSS, and the "intermediary" SSS.[8]

This model is used in which a multiparty CSD linked to the SSS transfers collateral from the secured securities issuer to the investment institution via an intermediary and receives it as collateral by the HCB (Figure A1.6).

Figure A1.6: Relayed Links

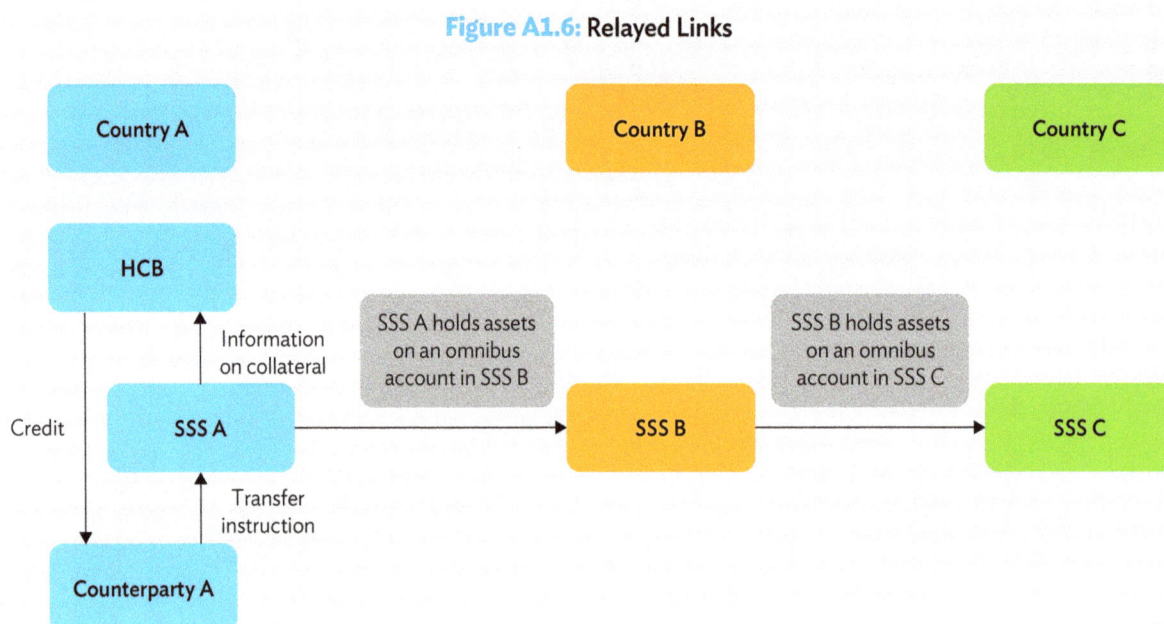

HCB = home central bank, SSS A = securities settlement system in Country A, SSS B = securities settlement system in Country B, SSS C = securities settlement system in Country C.

Source: European Central Bank. List of Eligible Links. Frankfurt. https://www.ecb.europa.eu/paym/coll/coll/ssslinks/.

3. Remote Access to Securities Settlement System

Under the Remote Access Model, both the HCB and its counterparty directly access a foreign-located SSS in which the collateral is available. The HCB accepts the collateral from its counterparties via the foreign-located SSS.[9]

The typical case is remote access to ICSDs such as Euroclear and Clearstream. Private-sector SSSs in some cases provide value-added services such as tri-party CMSs, so the HCB that uses the remote access model may be able to benefit from those additional services.

---

[8]   ECB. List of Eligible Links. Frankfurt. https://www.ecb.europa.eu/paym/coll/coll/ssslinks/; BIS. 2006. *Cross-border collateral arrangements*. Basel, pp. 26–27.

[9]   BIS. 2006. *Cross-border collateral arrangements*. Basel, pp. 24–25.

This model relies on the existing market infrastructure but requires that the HCB acquire significant knowledge about the functioning of foreign SSSs. Therefore, it may imply additional operational costs for the HCB. Besides, from an infrastructural perspective, an additional remote access link must be established and ongoing costs will arise from the use of the foreign SSS for both the HCB and financial institutions (Figure A1.7).

Figure A1.7: Remote Access to Securities Settlement System

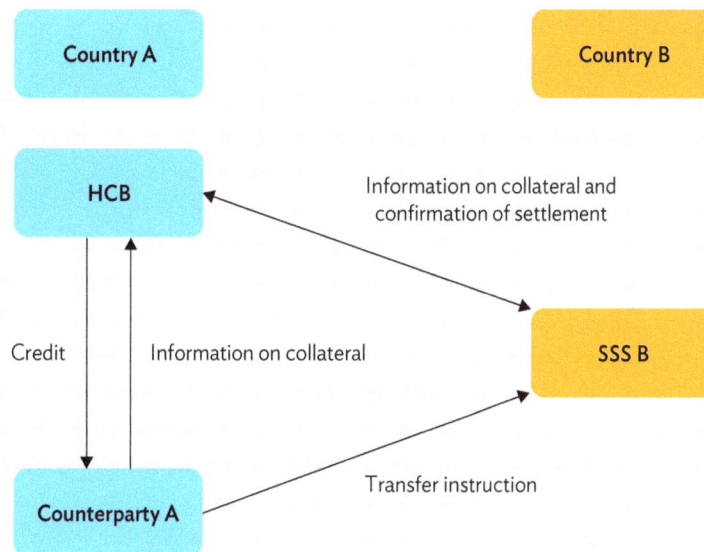

HCB = home central bank, SSS B = securities settlement system in Country B.
Source: Bank for International Settlements. 2006. *Cross-border collateral arrangements*. Basel.

SURVEY FOR PROMOTING THE USE OF LOCAL CURRENCY COLLATERAL FOR CROSS-BORDER FINANCIAL TRANSACTIONS

A. Summary of Survey Results

1. Overview of the Survey

The survey was aimed mainly at fact-finding regarding the regional bond market environment, identifying the challenges in the cross-border collateral market, exploring the appropriate policy measures, and collecting diverse views from Cross-Border Settlement Infrastructure Forum (CSIF) member institutions.

The survey was conducted from March to June 2021 among 27 institutions including central banks and central securities depositories (CSDs). Of the 27 institutions surveyed, 22 responses were collected. In particular, member institutions presented various opinions not only on their own bond markets but also on the regional bond markets as a whole.

2. Composition of the Survey Questionnaires

The questionnaire consists of a total of 30 questions under the five major categories.

- **Overview of local currency bond markets.** Bond transactions involving collateral by transaction types, such as repo, swap, securities lending, and other over-the-counter (OTC) derivatives, in terms of domestic market and cross-border markets, respectively.

- **Information on market infrastructures.** Detailed information for the financial market infrastructures (FMIs), such as real-time gross settlement (RTGS), CSD, and central clearing counterparty (CCP).

- **Impediments.** Situations that are being considered as constraints in facilitating cross-border collateral transactions.

- **Central bank collateral arrangement (CBCA).** Detailed information about the arrangements, such as what models and eligible bonds are used.

- **Existing and/or planned measures.** Policy actions that have been taken or scheduled to be implemented for promoting the cross-border collateral markets.

3. Summary of Survey Results

a. Local Currency Bond Market Environments

Local currency (LCY) bond issuances have been steadily increasing. This growing trend was bolstered mainly by government bonds, accounting for 71.8% of the total issuances as of 2020. However, the issuances were concentrated in a few economies, while the issuance volumes of other economies remain marginal. The trading volume of bonds surged during the process of responding to the global financial crisis. The increase in transaction volume since 2017 is largely attributable to the increase in bond issuance. All in all, the primary bond market is fairly large in size, but the trading volume of bonds has not increased that much, suggesting slow turnover ratios in the secondary market.

The collateral transactions demonstrate a continuous increase.[1] Among them, the most actively traded products that are well-known are repos. Although confined to the case of some member economies, the ratio of collateral transactions to total trading volume of bonds exceeded consistently above 80% during the 2018–2020 period.

b. Market Infrastructures

In most regional economies, CSDs and RTGS systems are put in place. Participation of market infrastructures is mostly limited to domestic financial institutions. However, some CSDs also allow direct participation of international CSDs (ICSDs). While domestic market infrastructures are well established, there are limited cases of linkages in place for cross-border clearing and settlement.

c. Impediments in Facilitating the Cross-Border Collateral Transactions

In order to identify constraints related to the cross-border collateral, eight questions were presented to the member institutions. Among these questions, the question regarding capital control measures had the highest frequency of responses at nine institutions. In following, the question regarding lack of public disclosure of relevant information had the next highest frequency at eight institutions (Figure A2.1):

- **Lack of local bond market development.** Some member institutions raised issues such as local bond markets in infancy, and lack of market makers and participants.

- **Insufficient transparency on laws and regulations.** The absence of a single platform to find information related to regulations for each economy and each economy's insufficient transparency were noted.

- **Capital control measures.** Restrictions on LCY bond transactions for cross-border, regulatory measures on capital movement, and complex pre-reporting procedures to foreign investors were reported.

- **Insufficient market infrastructures.** A few institutions mentioned by saying that their local FMIs only handle government bonds and that no local custodian services are available.

- **Insufficient disclosure of relevant information.** The level of disclosure of regulatory information is not satisfactory along with some language barriers being additional constraints.

---

[1]   In this study, collateral transaction was defined as financial transactions involving bonds as collateral. They include repos, swaps, securities loans, and other OTC derivatives transactions. Since this study is aimed at activating the use of local currency collateral for cross-border financial transactions, only bonds as collateral were analyzed.

Figure A2.1: **Number of CSIF Member Institutions Responded by Impediments**

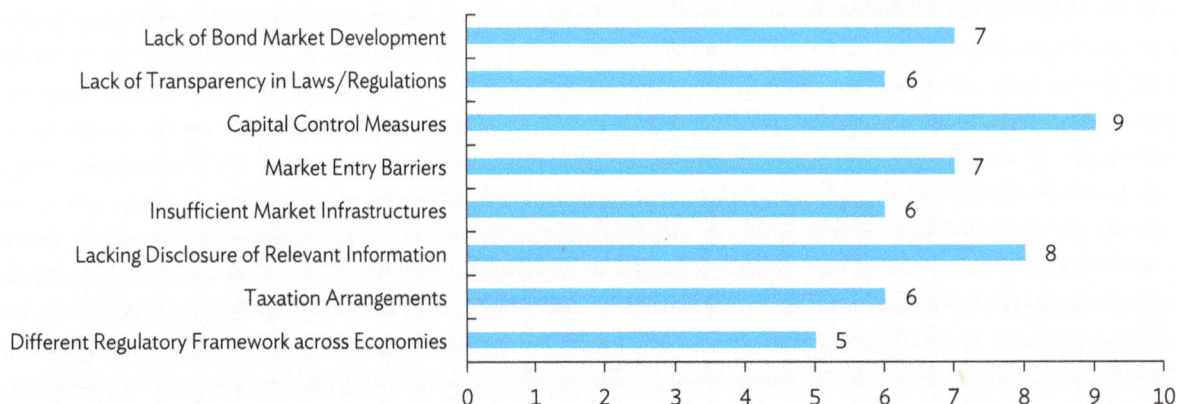

Lack of Bond Market Development	7
Lack of Transparency in Laws/Regulations	6
Capital Control Measures	9
Market Entry Barriers	7
Insufficient Market Infrastructures	6
Lacking Disclosure of Relevant Information	8
Taxation Arrangements	6
Different Regulatory Framework across Economies	5

CSIF = Cross-Border Settlement Infrastructure Forum.
Source: CSIF Survey (2021).

d. Central Bank Collateral Arrangement

It was observed that several central banks in the region have signed CBCAs that accept FCY bonds as collateral for lending. The Bank of Japan signed arrangements with three regional central banks: the Bank Indonesia, Bank of Thailand (BOT), and Monetary Authority of Singapore (MAS). In addition, three central banks—the Bank Negara Malaysia, BOT, and MAS—have signed bilateral arrangements with each other. They use the standard correspondent central banking model (CCBM) to implement CBCAs.

However, these arrangements currently adopted by regional central banks are rarely executed, partly reflecting the fact that such schemes were set up as one of the policy measures to address the turmoil in global markets.

e. Existing and/or Planned Policy Measures

The last section of the survey aimed at fact-finding regarding existing and/or planned measures to support cross-border collateral transactions in each economy.

Central banks that currently do not have a CBCA indicated the standard CCBM as the most likely model for use, should they need to consider the measure of the availability and ease of implementation based on incumbent market infrastructures.

Some member economies have linked their CSDs to ICSDs or have a plan to link in the future to support foreign investors. And some member economies are in the process of or in the plan to adopt ISO 20022 to support interoperability of market infrastructures. In addition, periodic meetings among authorities for development and establishment of the united off-exchange repo mechanism were suggested.

There are three bilateral Qualified ASEAN Bank (QAB) agreements among the Association of Southeast Asian Nations (ASEAN) economies. However, currently, only two QABs are in operation under the agreement between regional central banks.

B. Cross-Border Settlement Infrastructure Forum Survey Questionnaire

Survey for Promoting the Use of Local Currency Collateral for Cross-Border Financial Transactions

Member Jurisdiction

Please indicate your complete name and title (Mr. or Ms.)

Contact person
Designation
Institution
Country
E-mail address & Contact Number

Alternate person
Designation
Institution
Country
E-mail address & Contact Number

Notes:

CSIF colleagues (or experts) are encouraged to answer the following questions to the best extent possible.

CSIF, ADB does understand that this survey is an extremely demanding request, but strongly believes that this information collecting process is necessary to promote efficient and smooth cross-border collateral transactions for liquid and stable bond markets in ASEAN+3.

In this context, all CSIF members are invited to return a completed survey to the CSIF secretariat via e-mail by **23 April 2021**, using the contact information below.

E-mail: Yvonne Osonia (yosonia.consultant@adb.org) and Byung-Wook (Andrew) Ahn (bahn@adb.org).

Leelark Park
CSIF Consultant, ADB
E-mail: larkpark88@naver.com.

I. PURPOSE OF THE SURVEY

This survey is designed to collect information on the current environment surrounding collateral transactions within the Association of Southeast Asian Nations plus the People's Republic of China, Japan, and the Republic of Korea (ASEAN+3) member jurisdictions. The information and data collected through this survey would be utilized to lay the groundwork for the comprehensive research, which would be conducted for over 1 year in order to promote the use of LCY-denominated collateral for cross-border financial transactions.

Since the financial crisis, the bond market in the ASEAN+3 region has developed enormously in terms of size as well as quality, but it is still difficult to use quality securities in the ASEAN+3 region as cross-border collateral.

This study will rely heavily on fact-finding work. Statistics relating to bond issuances and transactions of member economies are already well organized in the *AsianBondsOnline* platform and relevant research. However, few studies have been conducted on cross-border collateral transactions in the region and, of course, the relevant data is very limited.

Therefore, CSIF believes that this survey is highly impactful and imperative in the process of the study. It would pave the way for successful fulfillment of CSIF initiatives that promote cross-border financial transactions.

Once again, CSIF kindly requests your kind support and assistance for taking a few steps forward in implementing the study.

After the in-depth analysis of the current environments involving regional collateral transactions, including identification of impediments through the survey, the next key activities would be focused on coming up with appropriate policy measures to improve the current status quo.

II. POTENTIAL BENEFITS FROM THE STUDY

In order to achieve market-based stability within the region, which is difficult to accomplish by national-level efforts, it is essential to expand adequate pools of collaterals throughout the region.

Furthermore, the use of adequate collateral for financial transactions, especially in cross-border transactions, is considered important in maintaining financial stability and promoting economic integration in the region.

By promoting the active use of LCY collateral for cross-border financial transactions, the following benefits are expected to be obtained.

a. Expanding the market instruments for obtaining the LCY liquidity from the local central bank and markets.
b. Facilitating the growth of the regional financial market by ensuring extra funding channels and reducing reliance on the US dollar.
c. Enhancing the credibility of the sovereign bonds by expanding eligibility of collateral pools.
d. Contributing to optimal allocation of global Investment portfolios, thanks to increased credibility of regional LCY bonds.
e. Strengthening financial stability in the region.

III. SURVEY ITEMS

A. Overview of the Local Currency Bond Markets

Please complete the following tables regarding the trading volume of bond transactions involving collateral by transaction types, and in terms of domestic market and cross-border markets respectively.

1. Trading Volume of the Bond Transactions involving Collateral (in Local Currency)

a. Domestic collateral transactions

	2020	2019	2018
i. Repo			
ii. Swap			
iii. Securities Lending			
iv. Other derivatives			
v. Total			
vi. % of Total Bond Transactions			

b. Cross-border collateral transactions*

*   This is a market where domestic quality debt securities denominated in LCY are used or accepted in cross-border collateral transactions. If you do not have the relevant data at your institution, it would be appreciated if your institution plays a coordinating role to compile relevant data.

	2020	2019	2018
i. Repo			
ii. Swap			
iii. Securities Lending			
iv. Other derivatives			
v. Total			
vi. % of Total Bond Transactions			

2. Repo Markets

a. Central Bank Repo

Type of Participants (both domestic and foreign by type of institution)
Eligible Collateral
Risk Management (haircut, margin call, mark-to-market)

b. Market-Based Repo

	OTC	Exchange
Type of Participants (both domestic and foreign by type of institution)		
Eligible Collateral		
Risk Management (haircut, margin call, mark-to-market)		

B. Market Infrastructure

Please fill in the table below with the information on each of the following market infrastructures respectively.

1. Real-Time Gross Settlement (RTGS)

i. Type of Participants (both domestic and foreign by type of institution)
ii. Eligibility criteria to be accepted as collateral*

*   Please describe the cases where the participants to this infrastructure need to post collateral, for example, (1) for urgent liquidity provision, (2) by internal regulations of the system operator, and (3) by risk-sharing arrangements to cover potential loss from participant defaults.

2. Central Securities Depository (CSD)

i.   Type of Participants (both domestic and foreign
     by type of institution)

ii. Eligibility criteria to be accepted as collateral*

* Please describe the cases where the participants to this infrastructure need to post collateral, for example, (1) by internal regulations of the
system operator and (2) by risk-sharing arrangements to cover potential loss from participant defaults.

iii. Interoperability*

* Is the system equipped with the capacity to be connected with other countries' CSD?
If yes, how is it implemented?
(1) by establishing direct linkage between foreign and domestic CSD
(2) through overseas custodian services
(3) by allowing foreign CSD to directly participate in the domestic CSD

3. Central Clearing Counterparty

i.   Type of Participants (both domestic and foreign
     by type of institution)

ii. Eligibility criteria to be accepted as collateral*

* Please describe the cases where the participants to this infrastructure need to post collateral, for example, (1) by internal regulations of the
system operator and (2) by risk-sharing arrangements to cover potential loss from participant defaults.

C. Impediments in Collateral Transactions

Each jurisdiction may have various constraints or obstacles in promoting the bond transactions.

Please provide all answers for the following situations that are being considered as impediments in facilitating collateral transactions on both the domestic market and the cross-border market.

For this section, CSIF believes that information from the key market players could contribute to preparing a more comprehensive answer.

1. Absence or Immature Growth (Development) of Bond Market
→ For example, there might be a situation where the financial market is not mature enough for the securities to be used as cross-border collateral. There also might be a case where the financial market is growing but the private sector's recognition of collateral is not mature enough.

Answer:

2. Lack of Transparency in Laws/Regulations
→ For example, market participants may find that domestic laws and regulations are unclear concerning how to deal with cross-border securities.

Answer:

3. Capital Control Measures

→ For example, if the cross-border use of collateral is counted as foreign capital inflow, there might be a case where private or public sectors' capacity to accept cross-border collateral is limited due to control measures over foreign capital. Please share if some restriction measures on foreign capital inflow could affect cross-border collateral activities.

Answer:

4. Market Entry Barriers

→ For example, there could be certain barriers hindering foreign institutions from entering the domestic market or participating in repo/other collateral transactions.

Answer:

5. Insufficient Market Infrastructures

→ For example, the current infrastructure may only be designed to handle domestic securities. It may need to be improved to handle cross-border transactions.

Answer:

6. Insufficient Transparency or Disclosure of Relevant Information

→ For example, market participant could find it difficult to access the necessary information to conduct collateral transactions due to a lack of transparency and disclosure.

Answer:

7. Taxation Arrangements

→ For example, some jurisdictions may impose taxes on interest income or capital gains from bond transactions while others do not.

Answer:

8. Differences in Legal/Regulatory Framework across Jurisdictions

→ For example, there might be a difference in the legal and regulatory frameworks among jurisdictions within the ASEAN+3 region. Please share some country-specific or idiosyncratic factors in your jurisdiction to be reconciled or considered in implementing cross-border uses of collaterals.

Answer:

9. Others

→ Please describe the situation where country-specific factors hinder the cross-border uses of LCY-denominated bonds.

Answer:

D. Cross-Border Collateral Arrangement (Central Bank Only)

Please provide detailed information of the arrangement for the use of LCY bonds as a cross-border collateral (CBCA*), such as what models and eligible bonds are used.

* CBCA is an institutional arrangement through which central banks could accept foreign collateral on a routine and/or emergency basis to support intraday and/or overnight credit for the market participants (Please refer to Section V).

1. Existing CBCA Models

* Or any other liquidity provision agreement with other jurisdictions using collateral securities.

Models*	Reason**	Please specify the details

* Please refer to Section V.
** Please describe reasons that your institution selected a particular type of CBCA.

2. Existing Eligible Collateral Criteria

Select one from the dropdown list	Please specify the details
Please choose	
Please choose	

3. Preferred CBCA Models in the Future

If you do not have any existing arrangements, please provide any information on models you are considering or prefer for future CBCA.

Models*	Reason**	Please specify the details

* Please refer to Section V.
** Please describe reasons that your institution selected a particular type of CBCA.

E. Fact-Finding of CSIF Jurisdictions' Existing and/or Planned Measures to Support Cross-Border Collateral Transactions

Are there any actions that have been taken since the global financial crisis or scheduled to be implemented for facilitating the cross-border collateral markets? If any, please provide details.

Purpose of Actions	Select *Yes* if taken or planned; otherwise select *No*	If *Yes*, please specify the details
Greater openness of the cross-border collateral market	*Please choose*	
Recognition of QABs* in your jurisdiction	*Please choose*	
Expansion of eligible collateral pool (repo, swap, securities lending, derivatives, etc.)	*Please choose*	
Establishment (or improvement) of market infrastructure	*Please choose*	
Tax reduction and/or exemption	*Please choose*	
Others (please specify)	*Please choose*	

* ASEAN Banking Integration Framework (ABIF) allows banks meeting certain criteria (Qualified ASEAN Banks or QABs) to have greater access to other ASEAN markets and more flexibility in operating in there. The QAB, under the ASEAN Banking Integration initiatives, is aimed at increasing openness of financial markets in the region. Given the nature of the QAB, it may have a positive effect on the increase of cross-border collateral transactions in the region, or putting it in an opposite way, cross-border collateral might be a catalyst for more active use of QAB.

IV. OTHER INFORMATION OR OPINIONS CONCERNING THE CROSS-BORDER TRANSACTIONS INVOLVING COLLATERAL

V. DESCRIPTION OF CROSS-BORDER COLLATERAL ARRANGEMENT MODELS

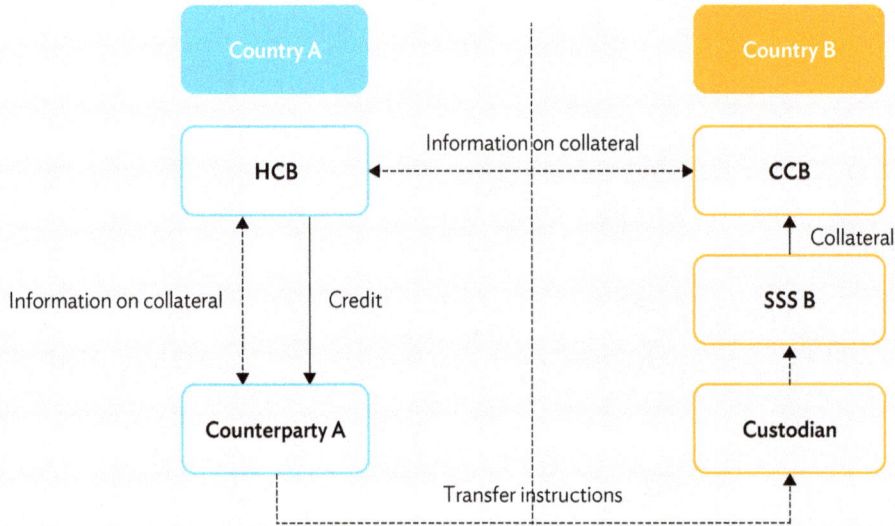

Figure A2.2: Correspondent Central Banking Model

CCB = correspondent central bank, HCB = home central bank, SSS = securities settlement system.

Note: Under this arrangement, national central banks act as custodians ("correspondents") for the HCB with respect to assets located in their local depository or SSS.

Source: Bank for International Settlements. 2006. *Cross-border collateral arrangements*. Basel.

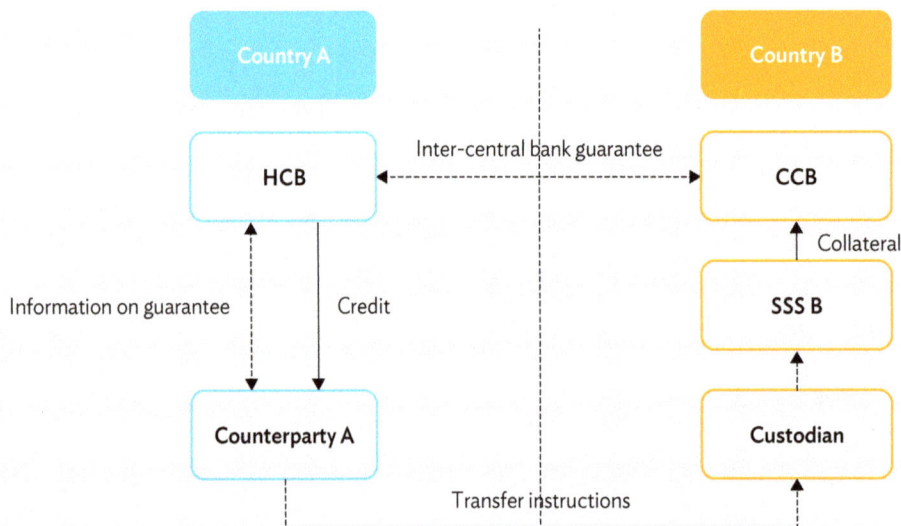

Figure A2.3: Guarantee Model

CCB = correspondent central bank, CCBM = correspondent central banking model, HCB = home central bank, SSS = securities settlement system.

Notes: Under this arrangement, national central banks act as guarantors for each other with respect to assets deposited in their local depository or SSS. Technically speaking, this model is similar to the CCBM described above. (It presents the same features as far as scope, implementation and feasibility are concerned.)

Source: Bank for International Settlements. 2006. *Cross-border collateral arrangements*. Basel.

Figure A2.4: Links between Securities Settlement Systems

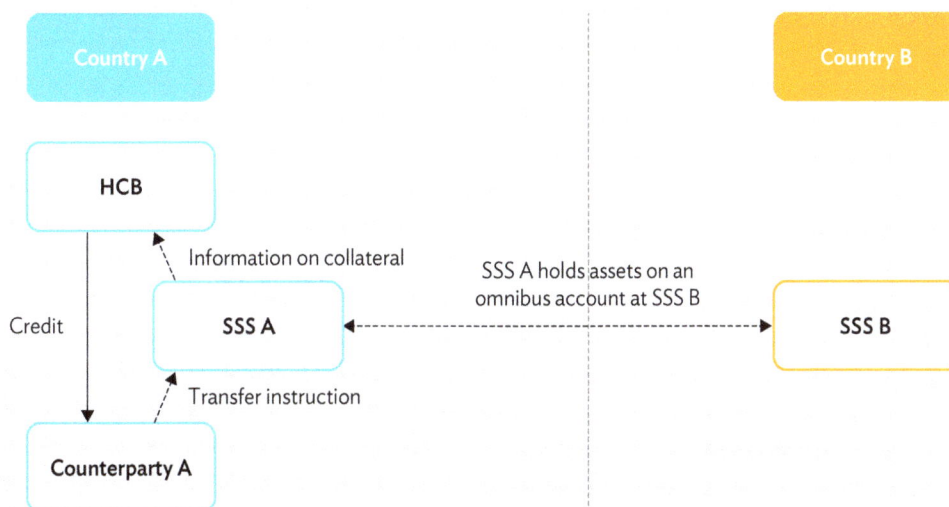

HCB = home central bank, SSS = securities settlement system.

Notes: Under this arrangement, the HCB and its counterparts use an SSS "linked" to one or more SSSs. A link between two SSSs allows a participant in one SSS to hold securities issued in another SSS without being a participant in the latter. With links, the cross-border relationship is between the SSSs: they open omnibus accounts with one another.

Source: Bank for International Settlements. 2006. *Cross-border collateral arrangements*. Basel.

Figure A2.5: Remote Access to a Securities Settlement System

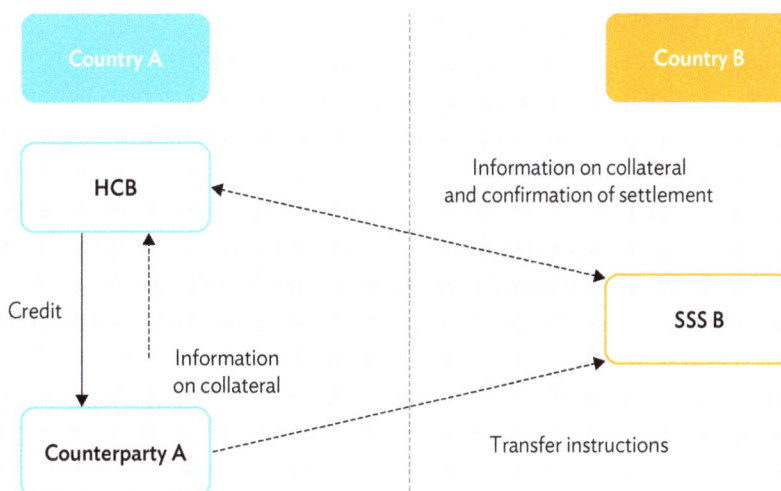

HCB = home central bank, SSS = securities settlement system.

Notes: Under this arrangement, both the HCB and its counterparties directly access a foreign-located SSS in which the collateral is available. An important variant of this model, often applied in practice, combines remote access with links, but the description below focuses on the remote access "building block" alone.

Source: Bank for International Settlements. 2006. *Cross-border collateral arrangements*. Basel.

Figure A2.6: Recourse to a Collateral Management System

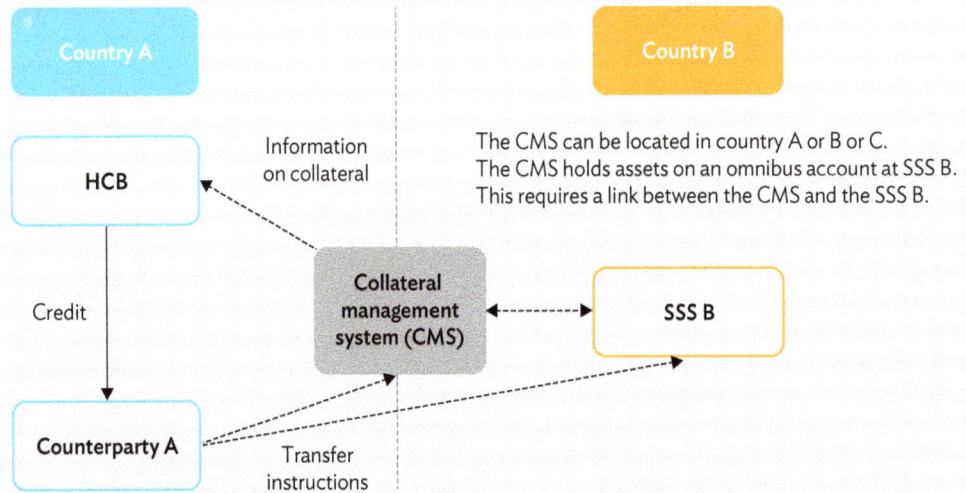

The CMS can be located in country A or B or C.
The CMS holds assets on an omnibus account at SSS B.
This requires a link between the CMS and the SSS B.

HCB = home central bank, SSS = securities settlement system.

Notes: Under this arrangement, the HCB and its counterparties rely on a CMS. The CMS can take the form of a collateral pooling system operated by a central bank, or a tripartite collateral service (pledge and/or repo) operated by an SSS or a custodian. Depending on the operator, the CMS could offer services for collateral issued in one or more countries. The CMS would become a global collateral pool if accessed by more than one HCB.

The CMS can be located in the home country of the HCB or abroad. In either case, the CMS has to open an omnibus account with the SSS in which the collateral is located (essentially a link between the CMS and the SSS). If the CMS were located abroad, the HCB would face similar legal and operational risks as for a case of remote access to an SSS. If the CMS were operated by another central bank, this central bank would have to open accounts not only for the HCB but also for its counterparties.

Source: Bank for International Settlements. 2006. *Cross-border collateral arrangements*. Basel.

www.ingramcontent.com/pod-product-compliance
Lightning Source LLC
Chambersburg PA
CBHW050049220326
41599CB00045B/7345